Mountain Biking

Michigan

The 50 Best Trails
And
Road Routes
In The
Upper Peninsula

PEGG LEGG
PUBLICATIONS

Other Biking Books From Pegg Legg Publications:

Mountain Biking Michigan:
The Best Trails In Northern Lower Michigan

Mountain Biking Michigan:
The Best Trails In Southern Michigan

Cycling Michigan:
The Best Routes In Western Michigan

Cycling Michigan:
The Best Routes In Eastern Michigan

Mountain Biking
Michigan

The 50 Best Trails
And
Road Routes
In The
Upper Peninsula

By Mike McLelland

U.P. Road Routes by
Karen Gentry

PEGG LEGG
PUBLICATIONS

Published by Thunder Bay Press
Production and design by Pegg Legg Publications
Maps by Pegg Legg Publications
Printing by Eerdmans Printing Company, Grand Rapids, MI
Inside photography by Mike McLelland and Karen Gentry
Author photos by Alison Engling

ISBN: 1-88-2376-57-9

3 4633 00122 6743

Printed in the United States of America

96 97 98 99 100   1 2 3 4 5 6 7 8

PEGG LEGG
PUBLICATIONS

Holt, Michigan

Acknowledgments

First and foremost, this book would not have been possible without Jim DuFresne, whose skill, motivation and expertise quarterbacked this project and took it from an idea during a dinner conversation to reality. Also, Karen Gentry wrote the road routes in this book and truly made this a comprehensive bicycling guide to the Upper Peninsula.

My parents, Bob and Joyce, and brother Rob were an inspiration during the research and writing of this book, as was Doug Megel. Without exception, every official from the state Department of Natural Resources and U.S. Forest Service I encountered helped me in any way they could and answered the sometimes simple and repetitive questions of a flatlander.

Also, thanks are due to the Michigan Mountain Biking Association, one of the most active and pro-active groups in the country. It would serve nicely as a model for any state hoping to further their mountain biking popularity.

Mike McLelland

Thanks to Mike McLelland, my former co-worker, who gave me the opportunity to contribute road routes to his mountain bike guidebook. I am indebted to my friend, Sandy Wilson, who graciously provided me with a home base in AuTrain, when I was wandering around the U.P.

Special thanks to Yoopers Dan Wilson and his co-hort Sonny Longtine for their enthusiasm and support of this project. Thanks to Bob DeYoung for his photo help. I would also like to thank Bob McCarty for some fun cycling adventures, including first tries at mountain biking and his friends (Ted, Rich and Barb) for riding the St. Ignace route. Thanks once again to my friends and family who put up with all my book and biking talk!

Karen Gentry

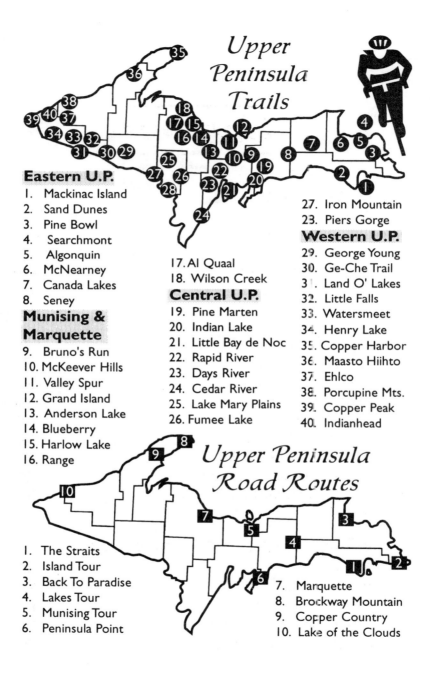

Upper Peninsula Trails

Eastern U.P.
1. Mackinac Island
2. Sand Dunes
3. Pine Bowl
4. Searchmont
5. Algonquin
6. McNearney
7. Canada Lakes
8. Seney

Munising & Marquette
9. Bruno's Run
10. McKeever Hills
11. Valley Spur
12. Grand Island
13. Anderson Lake
14. Blueberry
15. Harlow Lake
16. Range
17. Al Quaal
18. Wilson Creek

Central U.P.
19. Pine Marten
20. Indian Lake
21. Little Bay de Noc
22. Rapid River
23. Days River
24. Cedar River
25. Lake Mary Plains
26. Fumee Lake
27. Iron Mountain
28. Piers Gorge

Western U.P.
29. George Young
30. Ge-Che Trail
31. Land O' Lakes
32. Little Falls
33. Watersmeet
34. Henry Lake
35. Copper Harbor
36. Maasto Hiihto
37. Ehlco
38. Porcupine Mts.
39. Copper Peak
40. Indianhead

Upper Peninsula Road Routes

1. The Straits
2. Island Tour
3. Back To Paradise
4. Lakes Tour
5. Munising Tour
6. Peninsula Point
7. Marquette
8. Brockway Mountain
9. Copper Country
10. Lake of the Clouds

Contents

Central U.P.

Western U.P.

U.P. Road Routes

Map Symbols

This guidebook contains more than 60 maps, which use the following maps symbols:

Trailhead
or start of the ride

Lighthouse

U.S. Highway

Steep Hill

Picnic Area

Interstate

Waterfall

Park office

State Highway

Scenic View

Attraction

Swimming Area

Food Available

Campground

Rustic Campsite

Mountain bikers ride past the main frame of a mine shaft along the Mines & Pines Mountain Bike system in the Western Upper Peninsula.

Mountain Biking
The Upper Peninsula

I was cold, tired and lost. Near Hancock in the Keweenaw Peninsula, I was riding the labyrinth that is the Maasto Hiihto trail system, encountering few if any directional signs. Which gets back to being lost.

Demoralized by the lack of signage and countless spurs, all I wanted was to find my car when suddenly the sun popped out, brilliantly illuminating the limestone road I was following. That unexpected surprise was quickly exceeded by another when I pedaled over a rise and in front of me was a black bear, a large adult whose pitch-black coat against the crushed limestone was like a hole in the middle of the trail.

The bear was padding along with its head turned into an easterly breeze, totally oblivious of me. But squealing brakes got its attention and we stood, facing each other 30 yards apart, for what seemed an eternity. At first I thought about the camera in my fanny pack, but opted instead to simply enjoy what would surely be a fleeting moment. It was. The bear trotted into the undergrowth and I went back to exploring the woods from the seat of my mountain bike.

Only in the Upper Peninsula.

Only in this special region of Michigan can being lost and tired suddenly become the highpoint of an adventure. That's what mountain bikers have come to expect north of the Mackinac Bridge; an adventure, not just a ride.

That spirit of exploration is easy for any mountain biker to obtain in the U.P. The area is rugged, isolated by the Great Lakes, features awe-inspiring panoramas and some of the best off-road cycling in the Midwest. Only in the U.P. can you follow trails through old growth forests, be forced to carry your bike across a beaver dam, pause at the edge of a rocky bluff above a pristine lake, view a waterfall so close that it leaves a layer of mist on the handlebars. Best of all there's that sense of adventure, which comes from being the only one in the woods on a trail that is only lightly marked. You never know what's around the next bend but you're pretty sure it's not another biker because you haven't encountered one all weekend.

Is that a bear I see?

Mountain Biking In The U.P.

Why drive six or seven hours north when there is probably some single track 40 minutes from your home?

You come to the U.P. because you're tired of crowded trails, of scenery that amounts to farm fields and gravel pits, of trail systems that weave back and forth so much you pedal all day but never go anywhere. That's fine for everyday riding, as long as you spice it up once in a while with a weekend or longer up north.

It's important to understand, however, that for the most part trails in the U.P. were not designed for mountain biking. Many in this book were built to be enjoyed by cross country skiers under a three-foot layer of soft, powdery snow. Thus they will be wide paths with little regard for either wet areas or sand traps. Others are a network of old two-tracks and forest roads that will be crisscrossed by other old two-tracks and forest roads. Such situations have you stopping often and looking for trail signs. Still others are some of the most primitive single track in the Midwest.

In general, you will find mountain biking areas in the U.P. neither posted nor maintained as well as those in more developed areas of the state. Many are still easy to follow, others require a sense of route finding and some, like the Wilson Truck Trail in the

Huron Mountains, you better be packing a compass and a detailed topographical map. On any trail you should always be prepared to stop suddenly for fallen trees or low-hanging branches ready to separate your head from your shoulders.

U.P trails are not as technically challenging as their counterparts in southern Michigan in the sense of narrow single track that winds tightly around corners or weaves through a series of sudden dips. But the very nature of the terrain; hilly, rocky and unforgiving to those who lose control of their bikes, makes the area as challenging at times as anything you will encounter in Michigan.

Trails in the U.P. are vastly underused by mountain bikers. Compared to the pressure that trails at Yankee Springs and Pinckney recreation areas receive, well, there is no comparison. Another mountain biker on the trail is a rare sight, a trailhead parking lot full of cars is unheard of. That's why you drive six hours to ride here. But there is a flip side to that isolation on the trail. It means if you have a flat you can't count on a biker passing through with a tire pump. And if you get hurt, there's no quick relief.

Mountain bikers need to be aware of that and compensate by carrying the right equipment on long rides such as Grand Island or Ehlco Mountain Bike Comple. On such trips, a compass is an essential backcountry tool along with a bike repair kit, raingear, plenty of water and some high-energy snacks. It is also wise to check in with the park office or ranger district listed in each ride for the latest trail conditions and the most current map.

When To Ride

In southern Michigan, mountain bikers can often hit the trails by mid-April. This is hardly the case in the U.P., where the long, snowy winters mean a far shorter bike season. Traditionally the mountain biking season in the U.P. begins in late May, but if the winter has been especially hard the trail can still be a quagmire of mud then. In 1995, there was so much snow in the Porcupine Mountains Wilderness State Park that mountain bikers didn't start using the trail system until mid-June.

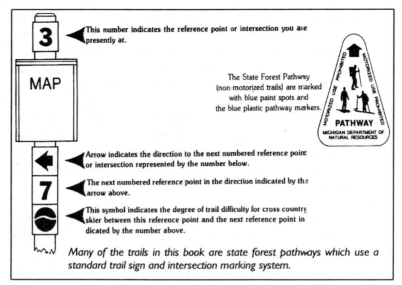

Many of the trails in this book are state forest pathways which use a standard trail sign and intersection marking system.

September and October are excellent months to ride, with fall colors setting in and caravans of road-hogging RVs finally gone from major roads like US-2. The first substantial snowfall usually occurs in early November and on Nov. 15, the start of the firearm deer season, it's time to store the bike for the winter. Yoopers take their deer hunting very seriously and would not look too kindly on a mountain biker who just chased an eight-point buck away from a bait pile. For all practical purposes the snowfall is too great and cross country skiing too popular to consider winter riding as is done in the southern half of the state.

Rules of the Trail

The International Mountain Biking Association has come up with six "Rules of the Trail" that all bikers should follow:

1. Ride on open trails only. Respect trail and road closures, private property, and requirements for permits and authorization. Federal and state wilderness areas are closed to cycling, and some park and forest trails are also off limits, particularly those in the dune areas along Lake Michigan and Lake Superior.

2. Leave no trace. Don't ride when the ground will be marred, such as after a rain. Never ride off the trail, skid your tires, or discard any object. Strive to pack out more than you pack in.

3. Control your bicycle. Inattention for even a second can cause disaster. Excessive speed frightens and injures people, gives mountain biking a bad name, and results in trail closures.

4. Always yield the trail. Make your approach known well in advance. A friendly greeting is considerate and appreciated. Show your respect when passing others by slowing to walking speed or even stopping. Anticipate that other trail users may be around corners or in blind spots.

5. Never spook animals.

6. Plan ahead. Know your equipment, your ability, and the area in which you are riding and prepare accordingly. Be self-sufficient at all times, keep your bike in good repair, and carry necessary supplies for changes in weather. Keep trails open by setting an example of responsible cycling for all to see.

The Michigan Mountain Biking Association also has a Responsibility Code:

1. Always yield the right of way to other trail users

2. Slow down and pass with care (or stop)

3. Control your speed at all times

4. Stay on designated trails

5. Don't disturb wildlife or livestock

6. Pack out litter

7. Respect public and private property

8. Know local rules

9. Plan ahead

10. Minimize impact

11. Avoid riding in large groups

12. Report incidents of trail impasse to local authorities

Trail Fees

Many trails have no riding fees whatsoever. State parks charge a vehicle entry fee, some mountain bike areas and ski resorts have a per-person fee and a growing number of national forest and state forest trail systems are being equipped with donation pipes at the trailheads.

Pay your fees. This is the era of "user pays" and if you want the trails open then we all must toss a few dollars in the pipe.

Trail Difficulty

The Trail Difficulty rating used in this book is a way to indicate the physical exertion required to ride the route. It's influenced by the elevation gain (length and steepness) and technical difficulty of a ride, including width and character of the trail, obstacles (roots, sand, etc.), and length of technical sections.

Easy: This is a relatively flat ride with very little elevation gain along a fairly wide trail or two-track. Most easy trails feature few if any sharp turns while uphill portions are short and gentle with grades of only four to seven percent.

Moderate: These trails include two-track and single track and often significant change in elevation as well as short technical sections. They usually require more endurance than technical skill and you will often encounter steep downhill runs and climbs.

Strenuous: These trails are rated for advanced riders for a variety of reasons; length, ruggedness of the terrain and difficulty in following them due to a lack of signage. Some trails, such as Grand Island, are rated strenuous because they are a true backcountry experience; miss the ferry back to Munising and you're going to spend a long night in the woods.

What trails should you ride and what should you avoid? Keep in mind an advanced biker is someone who can ride at least 15 miles and not get completely burned out, whatever the terrain. He or she can cover hills without hopping off the bike and can brake most of the time without skidding. They can manage trailside repairs or at the very least patch up their bike to get back to the trailhead.

The important thing is to enjoy yourself and for beginners that usually means avoiding the strenuous trails ... the main reason for

A mountain biker pauses to enjoy a waterfall, one of the special attractions of riding in the Upper Peninsula.

Ride	Location	Length	Surface
1. *Tranquil Bluff Trail*	Mackinac Island	9 miles	Single Track
2. *Sand Dunes Ski Trail*	St. Ignace	7.5 miles	Wide ski trail
3. *Pine Bowl Pathway*	Kinross	4.3 miles	Wide ski trail
4. *Achigan Cannonball*	Searchmont, Ont.	21.7 miles	Single & two-track
5. *Algonquin Ski Trail*	Sault Ste. Marie	9 miles	Wide ski trail
6. *McNearney Ski Trail*	Strongs	6.3 miles	Wide ski trail
7. *Canada Lakes Pathway*	Newberry	7.7 miles	Ski trail
8. *Seney Nat. Refuge*	Germfask	17.2 miles	Two-track
9. *Bruno's Run*	Munising	9.7 miles	Single track
10. *McKeever Hills Trail*	Munising	6.8 miles	Ski trails
11. *Valley Spur Ski Trail*	Munising	11.2 miles	Wide ski trails
12. *Grand Island*	Munising	22 miles	Single & two-track
13. *Anderson Lake*	Gwinn	4.5 miles	Single track
14. *Blueberry Ridge*	Marquette	13 miles	Wide ski trail
15. *Harlow Lake Pathway*	Marquette.	6.2 miles	Single & two-track
16. *Hill Street Trails*	Ishpeming	5 miles	Single & two-track
17. *Al Quaal*	Ishpeming	4.3 miles	Wide ski trails
18. *Wilson Creek Trail*	Big Bay	17.4 miles	Two-track
19. *Pine Marten Run*	Manistique	9.4 miles	Single & two-track
20. *Indian Lake Pathway*	Manistique	4.5 miles	Single & two-track
21. *Little Bay de Noc*	Rapid River	3 miles	Single track
22. *Rapid River Ski Trail*	Rapid River	9.7 miles	Ski trails
23. *Days River Pathway*	Gladstone	8.5 miles	Single track
24. *Cedar River Pathway*	Cedar River	7 miles	Single track
25. *Lake Mary Plains*	Crystal Falls	7.3 miles	Ski trail
26. *Fumee Lake*	Norway	8 miles	Single & two-track
27. *Iron Mt. City Park*	Iron Mountain	2 miles	Single track
28. *Piers Gorge Trail*	Norway	3 miles	Single track
29. *George Young*	Iron River	9.3 miles	Single & two-track
30. *Ge-Che Trail*	Iron River	11 miles	Single & two-track
31. *Land'O Lakes*	Watersmeet	8 miles one-way	Rail Trail
32. *Little Falls Rail Trail*	Watersmeet	12 miles one-way	Rail Trail
33. *Watersmeet Ski Trails*	Watersmeet	6.8 miles	Single & two-track
34. *Henry/Pomery Lake*	Marenisco	11 and 24 miles	Rail Trail & dirt roads
35. *Copper Harbor Pathway*	Copper Harbor	9 miles	Single track
36. *Maasto Hiihto Ski Trail*	Hancock	11 miles	Single & two-track
37. *Ehlco Complex*	Silver City	27 miles	Two-track
38. *Porcupine Mountains*	Silver City	12 miles	Wide ski trail
39. *Copper Peak*	Bessemer	12 miles	Ski flying hill
40. *Indianhead Resort*	Wakefield	7 & 3.5 miles	Downhill ski runs
41. *The Straits Tour*	St. Ignace	18 miles	Paved & gravel roads
42. *The Island Tour*	De Tour	65 miles	Paved roads
43. *Paradise Tour*	Paradise	74 miles	Paved roads
44. *The Lakes Tour*	Germfask	31 miles	Paved roads
45. *Munising Tour*	Munising	33 miles	Paved roads
46. *Peninsula Point Tour*	Rapid River	50 miles	Paved & gravel roads
47. *Marquette Tour*	Marquette	22 miles	Bike path and roads
48. *Brockway Mt. Tour*	Copper Harbor	32 mile	Paved roads
49. *Copper Country Tour*	Amheek	23 miles	Paved roads
50. *Lake of the Clouds*	Silver City	19.7 miles	Paved roads

Terrain	Difficulty	Comments
Steep bluffs	Moderate-Strenuous	Only way to escape the tourists
Forested dunes	Easy to Strenuous	Ten minutes from Mackinac Bridge
Level forest	Easy	Short drive from I-75
Hilly	Strenuous	Wilderness ride with train drop-off
Rolling forest	Moderate	Sand and wetlands
Rolling forest	Easy to Moderate	Lightly used by bikers
Rolling forest	Easy to Moderate	Scenic area with lakes
Level dikes	Easy	Wildlife viewing opportunities
Hilly	Moderate-Strenuous	Scenic lake country
Flat to rolling	Easy to Moderate	Connects to Bruno's Run
Rolling forest	Easy to Moderate	Ten minutes from Munising
Rolling forest	Moderate	Lake Superior cliffs and overlooks
Rolling forest	Easy to Moderate	Located at state forest campground
Rolling forest	Moderate	Very sandy trails
Hills and ridges	Moderate	Rental cabins along trail system
Hilly with bluffs	Easy to Strenuous	Scenic overlooks from rocky bluffs
Rolling	Easy	Ideal for families and beginners
Hills and ridges	Moderate-Strenuous	Adventure cycling on unmarked route
Hilly	Easy to Moderate	Free-use shelters for overnight rides
Flat to rolling	Easy	Excellent fall colors
Flat	Easy	Located at national forest campground
Forested dunes	Strenuous	Very hilly trail system
Rolling	Easy	Views of Days River
Flat to rolling	Easy	Located at state forest campground
Rolling	Moderate	Very lightly used system
Flat with one hill	Easy	Ride around scenic Fumee Lake
Rolling	Easy	Good trail for a workout
Flat to rolling	Easy to Moderate	Impressive gorge with rapids
Flat to rolling	Easy	Hot tub and pool for post-ride recovery
Hilly	Moderate-Strenuous	Adventurous backcountry ride
Flat	Easy	Crushed gravel rail trail
Flat	Moderate	Many swamps and marshes
Flat to rolling	Moderate	Lightly used system
Flat to rolling	Easy to moderate	Mostly dirt roads through lake country
Rolling to hilly	Moderate-Strenuous	Scenic bluff overlooks and virgin pines
Rolling to hilly	Strenuous	Confusing trail to follow
Rolling forests	Strenuous	Unbridged streams and beaver dams
Rolling to hilly	Strenuous	Virgin pines and waterfalls
Steep hill	Strenuous	Chair lift ride up, 30-mph run down
Steep ski hill	Moderate-strenuous	Wild downhill runs
Flat to rolling	Easy to moderate	Lake Michigan shoreline
Flat	Moderate	Views of Lake Huron islands
Flat	Moderate-strenuous	Option for a century ride
Flat to rolling	Moderate	Ride among northwoods lakes
Rolling	Moderate	Lake Superior shoreline and waterfalls
Flat	Moderate	Scenic lighthouse halfway point
Flat to rolling	Moderate	A ride around Marquette
Steep hills	Strenuous	Stunning views from Brockway Mt. Drive
Hilly	Moderate-strenuous	Lighthouse and Lake Superior views
Flat to rolling	Moderate	A ride-and-hike outing

this guidebook. The Mountain Biking Michigan series of guidebooks allow you to read about a trail in any part of the state in advance and then decide if you have the skill level to enjoy it, not just survive it. As your skills progress, you can begin tackling harder trails until you're riding with the best of them.

Finally, regardless of the trail difficulty, let others know where you are and when you expect to be back. This is especially true if you ride alone.

Michigan Mountain Biking Association

Michigan Mountain Biking Association is a statewide organization that was formed in 1990 to secure trails for off-road bikers and to oversee a series of quality mountain biking races in Michigan. Today there are more than a 1,000 members of MMBA and almost 30 bike shops that are MMBA sponsors.

To ensure the future of mountain biking in Michigan, join the MMBA and become active in your local chapter when it sponsors work parties and other events. For an application form write to MMBA, 2526 Elizabeth Lake Rd., Waterford, MI 48328.

Mountain Biking Tips

Heading north to the Upper Peninsula? Here are some mountain biking tips to make your trip safer and more enjoyable:

Parallel precaution - When coasting, keep your pedals parallel to the ground. If one pedal is at the bottom of a stroke, you could catch a tree root or other scrub and possibly break a toe or mangle an ankle.

Turn, don't burn - When turning on tight single track at speed try leaning your bike down and into the turn, while you stay upright, or perpendicular, to the trail. This can do two things - increase your control over the bike, and avoid spinning out in loose soil. To help with traction around corners, you can push your handlebars into the dirt, causing the knobby tires to bite in.

Rock on, baby - When climbing hills, it helps to rock front and back with your arms. When sitting, pull back and push forward with your arms as you pedal. You soon will find the rhythm.

Stand and deliver - During a hill climb sometimes it gets too hard to sit. When that happens, stand up - but there are some things you should be aware of. First, standing gives you an awful lot more power. Try to drop down a gear if you're going to stand to maximize your strength. Second, the tendency is to stand and hammer. But this drains your energy reserve. If you have to stand, try to avoid unnecessary jerking. Your off-seat climbing position should be just as controlled as your seated position.

The sandman cometh - You, like everyone else, will encounter sand, the mountain biker's worst nightmare. I used to tread through sand gingerly until I heard a guy in back of me downshift and motor past me. Now I hammer through it. Another important aspect of sand riding is to curve your spine backwards and roll it up over your rear tire. This will give you more say in your choice of lines through the sand.

Anticipation - Try to anticipate your gear changes before you need them.

Look ahead - Try to pick a 'line,' or path, within the trail that is easiest to traverse - the driest, the least bumps, etc. When climbing this is especially important because any bump or tree root will make you lose momentum, a precious commodity in the middle of a lung-sucker. Don't just look 20 feet ahead of you - look 20 yards, 30 yards, in front of you.

H20 - Drink plenty of water. The most remote regions of the Upper Peninsula are no place to suffer the downside of a dehydration episode. Make sure you drink plenty of water before, during, even after, you ride. Your body is a machine, keep it lubricated.

Pressure points - If your hands begin getting fatigued, relax your grip on the bars. The harder you squeeze on the bars the faster the muscles of your forearms and upper back will reach failure. Also, bar ends provide an excellent second and third position to grip (and rest).

Spin cycle - In general riding, and uphills, if you can get into the practice of pedaling circles instead of up and down you will be able to increase your efficiency. That's because there is no gap in power to the drivetrain.

The sweet spot - I have my favorite gear and you will find yours. If I am surprised by a hill, or encounter a sudden downhill, with one shift of the chainring I can be in either my favorite granny gear, or in the largest, gathering speed on a descent.

Feels bad, butt - When climbing the most obnoxious hills, I've found the best way to distribute your weight is to move up on the seat until the point is exactly where you don't want it. If the soil is right, you can get up the steepest stuff in this position.

Squeeze play - When traveling down hills stand up, hang your butt off the back of the seat, and squeeze the seat between your legs. This allows you more control of the bike by steadying its sway, and gives you another contact point with the bike.

Air awareness - Just because your tires say maximum pressure 65 lbs. doesn't mean you have to inflate them to that. You will find that if you keep the tire underinflated a bit it will give you better shock absorption on the trail. There usually is a range of pressure on the tire. But be careful not to under-inflate too much, as you will get a pinch flat, when the inner tube gets pinched between the tire and rim, and goes pssssst.

Practice makes perfect - Make sure you know how to perform simple bike maintenance, such as fixing a flat and adjusting derailluers, before you need to.

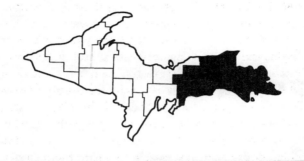

Eastern
Upper Peninsula

Mountain bikers ride a wooded trail toward Fort Holmes in the interior of Mackinac Island State Park.

Mackinac Island

County: Mackinac
Total Mileage: 30 miles
Terrain: Steep bluffs, hard-
wood forests and Lake
Huron
Fees: None
Difficulty: Moderate to strenuous

Mackinac Island, a 2,000-acre island just off St. Ignace, has
been known as a bicyclist's paradise ever since automobiles were
banned in 1896. The vast majority of cyclists arrive with road bikes
and follow M-184, the 8.4-mile road that skirts the edge of the
island and provides an endless view of Lake Huron.

But in recent years, more and more mountain bikers have
discovered the interior trails of Mackinac Island State Park, which
covers 83 percent of the island or 1,800 acres. In the middle of
the summer, when M-184 is overwhelmed with cyclists, in-line
skaters and horse-drawn carriages, you can escape the crowds
and find a bit of tranquility following these wooded trails.

There is little rhyme or reason in how the trails are laid out
and most of them are short segments, forcing you to stop often at
intersections and ponder which direction to head. Some trails,

like Manitou and Tranquil Bluff, are very technical rides but most of them are only moderately difficult. The trails with the greatest elevation change are those surrounding Fort Holmes, including Henry Trail, Beechwood Trail and Morning Snack Trail.

Keep in mind that some of the trails are either posted as horse-jumping routes with wooden posts across them or are used for guided rides by the local liveries. Please stay off them to avoid user conflicts between equestrians and the growing number of mountain bikers appearing each summer. The use of horses is a long and honored tradition on Mackinac Island, and any conflict will always end in their favor.

The route described below combines Tranquil Bluff Trail, the longest one on the Island at 3.8 miles, with a series of shorter trails to form a 9-mile loop from the downtown area. Most of the bicycle liveries in the downtown area are now renting mountain bikes but its still best to bring your wheels across on the ferry.

Getting There: You cannot drive on Mackinac Island, nor can you drive to it. Three companies provide ferry transportation from both the Upper and Lower peninsulas. From Mackinaw City, Arnold Transit (☎ 906-847-3351), Shepler's Mackinac Island Ferry (☎ 616-436-5023) and Star Line (☎ 906-643-7635) run the 8 miles across the straits from mid-May through mid-October. They also maintain ferries in St. Ignace and make that 5-mile trip from mid-April to early January.

Information: Near the ferry docks the park maintains a visitors center. For more information in advance contact Mackinac Island Historic State Parks, P.O. Box 370, Mackinac Island, MI 49757-0370; ☎ (906) 847-3328.

There is no camping on the island but there is a wide range of hotels, inns and bed-and-breakfasts. For a list of year-round accommodations call the Mackinac Island Chamber of Commerce at ☎ (906) 847-3783.

Tranquil Bluff Trail

Distance: 9 miles
Trail: Single track, two-track, paved road
Direction: Counter clockwise

This route begins with either the Winnebago Trail or the Manitou Trail. To reach their trailheads from the downtown area head east on Huron Street to Truscott Street. This paved road leads steeply up a bluff to some impressive summer homes along Huron Road (note that's Huron Road, not Huron Street) at the top. Head right on Huron Road to quickly pass the start of Winnebago Trail and then Manitou Trail a quarter-mile later where the road makes a sharp curve north.

The Manitou Trail is for expert mountain bikers only. Although only a half-mile long, this could be one of the most technical trails in the state. The narrow single track is filled with rocks, roots and sharp turns while skirting the edge of a 60-foot-high bluff. Make a mistake here and you pay a painful price. The trail ends at the parking area for carriages at Arch Rock.

Winnebago Trail is also rocky single track but doesn't skirt the sheer side of a bluff. An endo on this one results in a bruised arm, not a broken one. The trail extends 0.7 miles through a hilly forest to paved Arch Rock Road, where you turn right for a short ride to the Arch Rock parking area.

From Arch Rock, continue north on Leslie Avenue to pick up the start of Tranquil Bluff Trail. The first half of this single track also skirts a bluff that is not so tranquil and almost as rock-strewn as the Manitou Trail. Again, this is a trail that is more technical than most beginners can handle. If that's the case with you, it's easy to escape this stretch as the trail is constantly passing within sight of Leslie Avenue.

Tranquil Bluff Trail reaches the posted junction with Murray Trail at **Mile 2.4** and beyond it becomes considerably easier. You are still on the edge of the bluff but the sharp descents and climbs are gone. You quickly pass the posted Soldier's Garrison Trail, then emerge at Scott's Road just before **Mile 3**. Pick up Tranquil

Bluff Trail on the other side though it is not posted.

The trail begins as an easy, winding path but within a quarter mile you're faced with a short but steep climb. You top off at the edge of a bluff with a view of Lake Huron through the trees. For the next half mile you skirt this edge and enjoy more partial views of the water, and at one point even break out in a small clearing with Scott's Road below.

A steep, rocky descent is endured at **Mile 3.7**, with the trail continuing a more moderate downward trend beyond it. The single track becomes a wide path after passing Porter Hank's Trail and ends with a short downhill run to British Landing Road at **Mile 4.5**.

There are many ways to head back to the south end of the island, with Swamp Trail being the most natural choice when staring at a map. But this is a horse-jumping trail and should be avoided by mountain bikers.

The best route is to head right (north) or British Landing Road and then right again on Scott's Road, a narrow gravel road. If you continued straight on British Landing Road to its junction with M-185, there is a picnic area along Lake Huron with bathrooms, drinking fountains and a refreshment stand.

Scott's Road remains gravel for the first mile, something of a relief for many people after Tranquil Bluff Trail. You pass Scott's Shore Road and then begin climbing steeply, topping out at the junction with Tranquil Bluff Trail at **Mile 6**. In another half mile you arrive at Leslie Avenue, where Scott's Road ends. Straight ahead is Scott's Trail, a narrow single track, reached at **Mile 6.8**.

In this final leg of the ride the trails are short, mostly unsigned and very confusing. Don't worry. Ride a half mile in any direction and you'll break out at a major road that will lead you back to civilization, i.e. the pubs and bars in the downtown area.

Within a third of a mile Scott's Trail arrives at Crooked Tree Road, a two-track, and continues on the other side as a narrow single track in the woods. You quickly arrive at a junction with another trail, Juniper Trail, but it's unposted. Hang a right and then

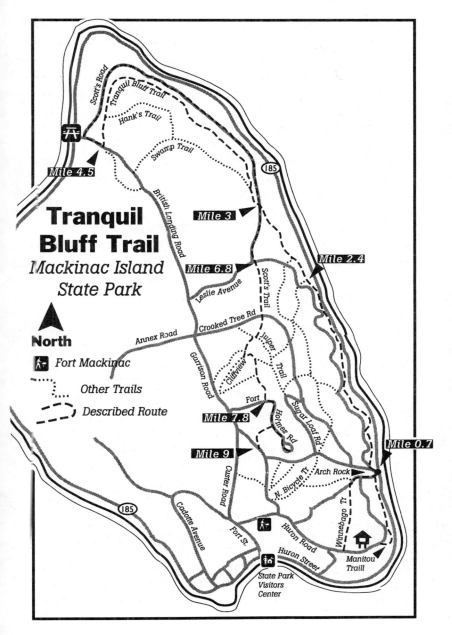

Tranquil Bluff Trail

Mackinac Island State Park

North

Scott's Road
Tranquil Bluff Trail
Hank's Trail
Swamp Trail
British Landing Road
185
Mile 4.5
Mile 3
Mile 2.4
Mile 6.8
Leslie Avenue
Scott's Trail
Annex Road
Crooked Tree Rd
Juniper Trail
Cliffview
Garrison Road
Fort
Haines Rd
Sugar Loaf Rd.
Mile 7.8
Mile 9
Mile 0.7
Arch Rock
N. Bicycle Tr
Custer Road
Winnebago Tr
Manitou
Traill
Cadotte Avenue
Fort St.
Huron Road
Huron Street
State Park
Visitors
Center
185

Fort Mackinac

..... Other Trails

- - - Described Route

a quick left to continue in a southerly direction on Cliffview Trail. Shortly you will pass a trail marker pointing up a steep climb posted as Morning Snack Trail. Where they come up with these trail names, I have no idea.

The climb is a grunt at first but once on top the ridge levels out somewhat, passes a junction with Beechwood Trail and then breaks out onto Fort Holmes Road at **Mile 7.3**. It's not quite a half mile along the road to Fort Holmes itself. The fort is the highest point of the island and the spot where the British set up a six-pound cannon and re-took the Island from the Americans in 1812 without firing a shot. There are great views from this spot and interpretive plaques explaining the history behind it.

After soaking up the scenery, backtrack along the road to Henry Trail on the left-hand side. This is basically one long downhill run along a badly rutted trail. Be careful! You end up on Garrison Road, next to Skull Cave, not much more than a half mile from the downtown area.

Sand Dunes Ski Trail

County: Mackinac
Total Mileage: 9.5 miles
Terrain: Forested dunes and
patches of sand
Fees: Donations
Difficulty: Easy to strenuous

Just up the road from the Mackinac Bridge is Sand Dunes Cross Country Ski Trail, a great system that fulfills the expectations of any mountain biker, no matter your skill level. The trail is located in the forested dunes of the Hiawatha National Forest and is composed of seven loops that total almost 10 miles.

If you're a novice, hit the eastern loops, particularly the flat A Loop, a ride of 1.5 miles. If you want to test yourself on downhill runs called Feeling Lucky and Holy Cow, jump on loops F and G. There is sand on this trail - the hills are sand dunes - but not so much that it's unbearable.

A nice advantage of this trail is its proximity to the Mackinac Bridge. If you're heading west on US-2, the St. Ignace Ranger Station is conveniently passed within minutes of the bridge and is the place to pick up a trail map Monday through Friday from 8 a.m. to 5 p.m. The trail is just another 5 miles west off of US-2.

If you're coming home after a weekend or a week of mountain biking in the U.P., this trail offers one last opportunity for a ride before crossing the Mighty Mac and beginning that long drive south.

Getting There: From the Mackinac Bridge, head west on US-2 for 11 miles and then north on Brevoort for a half mile. The trail is posted along US-2.

Information: Contact the St. Ignace Ranger District, US-2, St. Ignace, MI 49781; ☎ (907) 643-7900.

Sand Dunes Cross Country Ski Trail

Distance: 7.6 miles
Trail: Single track and two-track
Direction: Counter clockwise

At the trailhead is a parking area, a donation canister and a log warming hut for cross-country skiers. The trail begins next to the cabin as a single track but quickly turns into a two-track in a forest of mostly maple and aspen. At the first intersection head straight to continue onto Loop B. Loop A, the easiest route, swings left here eventually leading back to the trailhead in 1.5 miles.

Loop B immediately becomes more hilly as you climb a ridge with wetlands and large ferns on each side. Within a quarter mile of the junction the trail splits around a short, steep uphill to the top of a ridgeline. At **Mile 1** the trail splits again, offering a nice run down the slope called Omigosh. An equally hard down-and-up segment called Wildcat follows and then the posted intersection to Loop C is reached at **Mile 1.2**. Veer right.

Loop C is more overgrown, and you'll tighten your grip for Get Down, a downhill which bottoms out in mixed pines. Here the trail becomes a narrower version of itself, so minimal at times it feels like you're cutting your way through the forest. At **Mile 1.4** is the most significant uphill of the first three loops. The grade isn't that bad, but the white sand makes for heavy pedaling.

The trail does a lot of bobbing and weaving in the pine forest, where your chances of seeing a deer are good. Just beyond **Mile 2** is the intersection to continue onto Loop D. Veer right to stay on the peripheral route. Soon after the intersection veer left at a fork and again at a fork at **Mile 2.5** to stay on main trail.

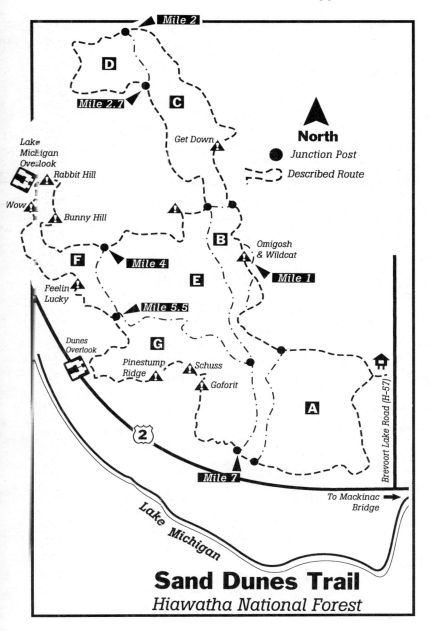

After a couple of rather steep down-and-ups you return to Loop C at an intersection at **Mile 2.7**. Hang a right and soon the forest opens to a view while the trail levels out for a leisurely pedal. The easy riding ends at **Mile 3**, when a significant uphill will get your heart pumping again. The payback is a nice little downhill that takes you across a ridge. At **Mile 3.5** is the intersection for Loop E. Veer right along a trail that is a little wider and not as sandy. There is still a bit of a roll along this segment.

Loop F, the most difficult portion of the route, is reached at **Mile 4**. It doesn't look that way at first because Loop E is a climb into the Eollan Hills and Loop F starts out flat. But soon the back loop becomes a lot more rolly, with sharper angles and geography. You're either pedaling uphill or coasting downhill for almost the entire 1.5-mile run.

If you have the legs for it this is an excellent part of the trail system. At **Mile 4.3** you hit Bunny Hill, a pretty steep downward coast. The ensuing Rabbit Hill is not as steep, but longer. At the bottom look for the blue diamond and take a right at the intersection. A narrow, steep uphill connects you back on the main trail.

The first glimpse of Lake Michigan comes right before **Mile 5**. US-2 cuts through your line of vision, with about 100 yards of dunes to the lakeshore, but you won't even know the highway is there unless a truck rolls by. Another steep downhill quickly follows. If you're squeamish about steep angles, there's a bypass here. If you took it, congratulations! Now you're ready for the most challenging downhill of the day, Feeling Lucky, just down the trail.

At **Mile 5.5** is the intersection in which you continue straight to ride Loop G. Shortly you'll notice the hills becoming smaller and at **Mile 6** there is a spur to Dunes Overlook. After that it's back to work, as you climb and ride across Pinestump Ridge, a narrow ridgeline with a few bypasses for the steeper downhills. The terrain here appears as if this part of the earth froze in mid-boil.

At **Mile 7** is the final intersection and a return to Loop A. From here it is an easy pedal back to the car and your favorite refreshment.

Pine Bowl Pathway

County: Chippewa
Total Mileage: 6 miles
Terrain: Mature forest and meadows
Fees: Donations
Difficulty: Easy

Driving through Kinross, with its numerous correctional facilities, is an interesting contrast to the freedom mountain bikers seek out in the forests and landscapes of the U.P. Kinross is home to the Kinross Correctional Facility, Hiawatha and Chippewa temporary correctional facilities, and the Chippewa Regional Correctional Facility. All that chain link and razor wire may tempt you to press harder on the accelerator, but this is one place with a constant reminder to obey the posted speed limits.

Located nearby is the Pine Bowl Pathway, an excellent little ride of 4.3 miles. Although there are lots of terrain changes and chop in this state forest pathway system, you barely notice the blips in elevation as you pedal along. The only problem is that this trail is one of the shortest described in this book and you may have to ride it over again to get a good workout.

Getting There: The pathway is 16 miles south of Sault Ste. Marie. From I-75, depart at exit 378 and head east on Tone Road for 4 miles. Turn south on Wilson Road and the trailhead will be reached within a mile.

Information: Contact Lake Superior State Forest, P.O. Box 77, Newberry, MI 49868; ☎ (906) 293-5131.

Pine Bowl Pathway
Distance: 4.3 miles
Trail: Single track and two-track
Direction: Counter clockwise

You enter in a pine plantation and immediately encounter Post 2. Veer right for Post 3, reached at **Mile 0.8**, and be prepared for some hoof prints on the single track as equestrians use the system as well. At Post 3 you have the first opportunity to return to the trailhead for a 2-mile ride.

At this point the trail is a gentle spin over last fall's leaves until you bottom out in a stand of pines and Post 3A. For those who want to ride the full 5.7 miles you'll have to continue to Post 3B. This ride heads straight to Post 4 for a 4.3-mile route.

This trail crosses other trails but blue blazes on the trees will keep you on course. At **Mile 2.4** you pass evidence of a fire, the reason for the open views and sparse vegetation, and then follow a ridge that provides views of the surrounding landscape.

A quarter mile later the trail develops a chop as it winds through a mature stand of pine and then climbs another ridge, where the forest changes to mature aspen and maple. The trail widens to a two-track and at **Mile 3.2** Post 5 and a bench are reached. Beyond Post 5 you spin along the edge of a pine plantation and then reach Post 6. Head left here to return to the trailhead and the parking lot.

Past the sixth post you veer right at Wilson Road to stay on the trail and then left just past an intersecting two-track. Eventually the pine stand opens into a meadow beyond the road and then you pass a Christmas tree farm before reaching the trailhead on this 4.3-mile ride.

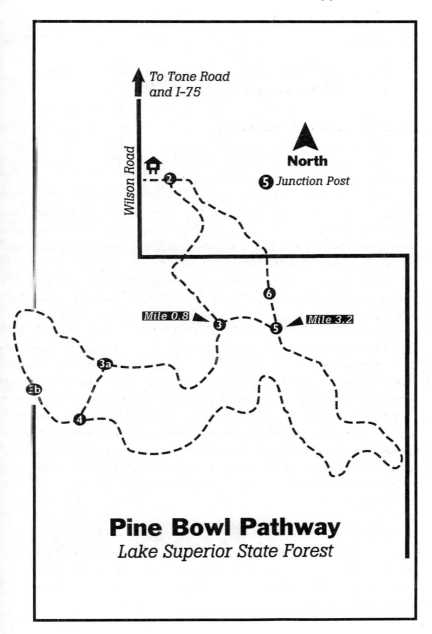

To Tone Road and I-75

Wilson Road

North

5 *Junction Post*

2

6

Mile 0.8 ▶ **3**

5 ◀ Mile 3.2

3a

3b

4

Pine Bowl Pathway
Lake Superior State Forest

A mountain biker loads her bicycle onto the baggage car of the Algoma Central Railroad for a trip to a wilderness trailhead. Her ride along mining trails and logging roads ended back at Searchmont Ski Resort.

Searchmont Ski Resort

Province: Ontario
Total Mileage: 124 miles
Terrain: Wilderness lakes, waterfalls, old mine ruins
Fees: Trail fee
Difficulty: Moderate to strenuous

Mountain bikers of Michigan are slowly discovering the place they call the Mountains of the Midwest. Just a short drive north of the International Bridge and Sault Ste. Marie are steep ridges and peaks, wilderness lakes, and miles of old logging roads that have been posted and mapped out by Searchmont Resort.

In other words, a mountain biker's paradise.

More than 124 miles of trails wind through a wilderness area so remote that most of the trailheads cannot be reached by car. Instead you hop on the Algoma Central Railroad (ACR), the famous Snow Train of Agawa Canyon. And it's that aspect of the adventure, taking a train to the middle of nowhere, that initially attracts most mountain bikers to the area.

Although Searchmont stages a number of organized rides throughout the year, including the Red Maple Ride that corresponds to the fall colors in September, the trail system is open anytime from mid-May through October, when the first snowfalls end another cycling season. Riders can either show up at the resort office and pay a trail fee or call Searchmont (☎ 800-663-2546) for an entire mountain biking package that includes lodging, meals, trail passes and a map. The resort even has bike rentals and biking guides.

Searchmont has divided its trails into three general groups. The Resort Trails are easy trips from the lodge along the Searchmont cross country ski trails or on nearby roads. The Goulais River System is trails and road routes to the northeast of the resort that include single track to the beautiful Goulais River Falls. The Achigan Circle system are the trails north of the resort best reached with a trip on the ACR.

Searchmont is constantly upgrading the system and re-routing parts of it so it's important to double check trail conditions before heading out. Most trailheads and junctions are marked with a number on blue metal attached to posts or trees, which correspond to the resort's trail map. Keep in mind, however, this is backcountry riding and you need to carry water, high energy snacks, insect repellent, compass and map and the proper bike repair kit.

Timid two-wheelers can rest easy in the knowledge that there are several double track routes near the resort or to scenic waterfalls along the Goulais River that are easy to follow and don't involve the Algoma Central Railroad.

On the other end of the spectrum, however, is the Mekatina Trail. The adventure begins by riding the local train to Mile 70, then continues with a three- to four-hour bike ride through a remote area of lakes, ridges and swamps. It ends at Mile 53 of the Algoma Central Railroad, where you flag down the train for a trip back to civilization.

Don't be late, sleeping in Spandex can get cold at night.

Getting There: Searchmont is a six-hour drive from southern Michigan. From Sault Ste. Marie in Michigan, cross the International Bridge into Sault Ste. Marie, Ontario, and head north out of town on Highway 17N. Within nine miles turn right on High-

A mountain biker skirts around a lake while following the Achigan Cannonball Trail back to Searchmont Ski Resort in the Algoma highlands region of Ontario.

way 556 and follow the signs to the ski resort.

Information: Contact Searchmont Resort, P.O. Box 1029, Sault Ste. Marie, Ontario, Canada P6A 5N5; ☎ (800) 663-2546.

Achigan Cannonball

Distance: 21.7 miles
Trail: Single track and forest roads
Rating: Strenuous

This is a wilderness adventure that the staff at Searchmont simply call "the Legend." The 21.7-mile route is a challenging ride for advanced mountain bikers as it includes many stretches of technical single track, the most noted being the Gonzo Trail.

Begin the adventure at the Searchmont Train Depot to catch the 10:30 a.m. northbound train along with the usual passengers of hunters, anglers and locals trying to get to some remote cabin. It's best to double check the train schedule the night before for possible seasonal changes. Purchase your ticket from the train conductor, and tell him you want to get off at Lower Achigan Lake at Mile 42.

Put your bike into the baggage car and then head for a passenger car and enjoy the scenery as the train rumbles north. It takes about 20 to 30 minutes to reach Achigan Lake, which is Post 14 on mountain bike maps handed out at the resort.

At the Achigan Lake train stop, unload the bikes from the baggage car and head left at Post 18 to pick up Pike Lake Trail. Within a third of a mile bear right. The old logging road starts through mixed forest and passes a small lake before becoming more of a trail that twists and turns to an old gravel pit. Here Post 22 marks a short spur to an overview of Pike Lake. At **Mile 3.7**, Pike Lake Trail ends at Post 17 along the Achigan Circle Trail.

Veer right onto Achigan Circle to pass a pair of ponds and reach Post 9 at **Mile 5**, which marks the Christina Mine Trail. This trail is an old narrow-gauge railroad bed that climbs steadily for more than 2 miles to Christina Lake, the high point of the day at

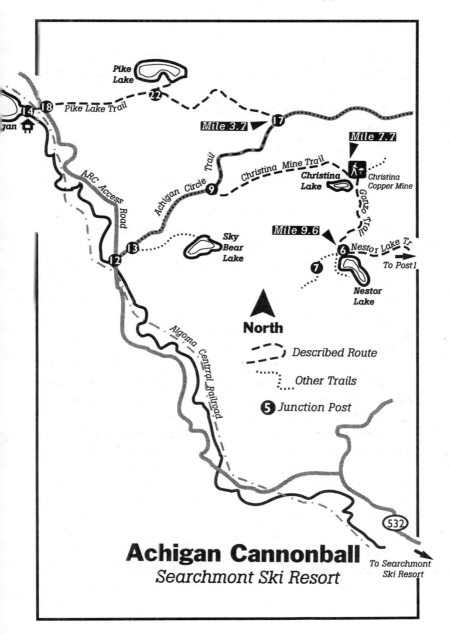

Pike
Lake

22

14 **18** Pike Lake Trail

gan

Mile 3.7 ▼ **17**

Mile 7.7 ▼

ARC Access Road

Achigan Circle Trail

9 Christina Mine Trail

Christina
Lake

Christina
Copper Mine

Gonzo Trail

13

Sky
Bear
Lake

Mile 9.6 ▼

6 Nestor Lake Tr.

7

To Post 1

12

Nestor
Lake

▲

North

Algoma Central Railroad

Described Route

Other Trails

5 Junction Post

532

Achigan Cannonball
Searchmont Ski Resort

To Searchmont
Ski Resort

more than 1,400 feet.

The lake and mine ruins, reached at **Mile 7.7**, are a tranquil spot, ideal for an extended break. The railroad was built in 1905 to carry copper ore from the Christina Mine down to the Algoma Central Railroad, the main line. Eventually the ore was shipped to Pittsburgh for refining. The mine was closed after six years because its owner had the unfortunate luck of booking passage on the Titantic's maiden voyage. Today you can peer down the old mine shafts, of which the main one is 400 feet deep. Also visible nearby is a huge boiler and along the trail, a 100 yards before the lake, is an old log cabin.

The next leg is the Gonzo Trail, a wild downhll run that lasts for almost 2 miles. From the mine site head left to pick up the narrow single track that winds behind the pile of copper tailings. Here a narrow, natural causeway leads to the trail. Be aware that the Gonzo is a rutted trail filled with large rocks. logs and small streams. Most mountain bikers must dismount more than once before reaching the end of it at Post 6. The junction is reached at **Mile 9.6**. Head left along the Nestor Lake Trail.

Nestor Trail is a forest road that makes a gradual descent east and crosses three streams along the way. Within a half mile you pass a beaver pond with a pair of impressive dams on the south side of the trail that you can stop at and check out. From the dams it's a mile and half to Post 1 on Achigan Circle Trail, reached at **Mile 11.8**. Once back on Achigan Circle head right (south) for the next 2.5 miles to reach Post 20.

At this junction you pick up the Up-Over-And-Down Trail, a challenging stretch that connects the Achigan Crcle with the Goulais River Trail. The first half mile is easy but then the trail becomes a technical single track that twists and turns uphill for the next 2 miles. The single track ends at the bridge over Perry Creek and beyond it is Post 15, reached at **Mile 17**.

Continue right here to reach Whitman Dam Road at **Mile 18.6**. You're now only 3 miles from the resort and an ice cold beer. Whitman Dam Road quickly turns into a paved road and

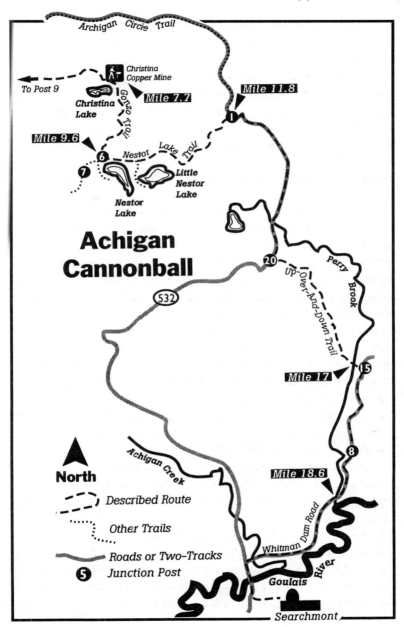

To Post 9

Archigan Circle Trail

Christina Copper Mine

Mile 7.7

Christina Lake

Gonzo Trail

Mile 11.8

Mile 9.6

Nestor Lake Trail

Nestor Lake

Little Nestor Lake

Nestor Lake

Achigan Cannonball

532

Perry Brook

Up-Over-And-Down Trail

Mile 17

Mile 18.6

Achigan Creek

North

- - - *Described Route*

.... *Other Trails*

──── *Roads or Two-Tracks*

5 *Junction Post*

Whitman Dam Road

Goulais River

Searchmont

heads west to end at Hwy 532. Once on Hwy 532 Searchmont Resort is just a short ride to the south.

Achigan Circle

Distance: 20.4 miles
Trail: Some single track but mostly two-track and logging roads
Rating: Moderate

This route is an easier version of the Achigan Circle as it skips both the Gonzo and Up-Over-And-Down Trails but includes the best scenery. You begin with a train ride to Achigan Lake and follow the same route to Christina Mine as described above.

When you're done inspecting the mining ruins, bypass the Gonzo Trail and backtrack along the Christina Mine Trail to Post 9 on the Achigan Circle Trail. This time the ride will be a very pleasant downhill run that lasts for more than 2 miles. At Post 9, veer right to continue on the Achigan Circle for the next 2 miles.

At **Mile 10.5** you reach Post 10 at the ACR Access Road, a rough dirt road. Shortly you will be crossing the Algoma Central Railroad and continuing south on its west side. From here its 3.7 miles to Station Bridge over Achigan Creek and then less than 2 miles to Hwy 532, reached at **Mile 14.5**. Hwy 532 is then followed south back to Searchmont Resort.

Mekatina Trail

Distance: 17.3 miles
Trail: Forest road and single track
Rating: Very strenuous

This is one of the most adventurous trails out of Searchmont. You begin by taking the Algoma Central Railroad to Mekatina Crossing at Mile 70. At this remote stop you head west along a forest trail that within 3 miles widens into a two-track. In the next 9 miles the route loops south, passing several lakes, climbs many ridges and crosses a bridge over McDonald Creek. Once across the creek, you're 5 miles from the Algoma Central Railroad at its Mile 53 crossing. Flag down the southbound train for a ride back

to Searchmont.

Advanced mountain bikers can cover this route in three to four hours if they know the area. If you don't, then obtain detailed topographical maps and the latest trail instructions from Searchmont Resort. Pack along emergency supplies and equipment and then set aside the day to cover the route so there is little chance of missing the last train.

For mountain bikers Algonquin Ski Trail can be a very wet and sandy outing at times though areas are bridged. To avoid the worse segments of sand, begin your return ride at Post 12.

Algonquin Ski Trail

County: Chippewa
Total Mileage: 10.3 miles
Terrain: Forests, wetlands, sandy hills
Fees: Donation
Difficulty: Moderate

Although called a cross country ski trail and built for skiers in the mid-1980s, Algonquin is actually a multi-use pathway open to hikers and mountain bikers as well. The majority of the terrain is flat and overall this would be easy riding if it wasn't for the sand in the second half of this 10.3-mile system.

The first half of this trail, however, is excellent. The riding is easy and the scenery is a refreshing diversion from the standard U.P. mixed hardwood. The first three loops offer plenty of wetlands, where the vegetation is lush, the smells are woodsy and wildlife viewing opportunities plentiful.

If you want to escape the heavier sand, then simply head over to Post 12 from Post 6 and begin the return trip. If, on the other hand, you are more aerobically-inclined, want a strenuous workout, or for some reason gravitate to sand for punishment, follow the complete outside loop of this system for a 9-mile ride.

Bisecting this trail system in half is the Soo-Strongs Rail Trail, which extends 32 miles from the west side of Sault Ste. Marie to the hamlet of Strongs. In the winter the raised bed of this former railroad is used by snowmobilers but in the summer it can provide miles of additional riding for mountain bikers.

Getting There: From I-75, depart at the Three Mile Road exit, two miles south of Sault Ste. Marie. Head west on Three Mile Road for a mile and then north on Baker Road and west on 16th Avenue. The trailhead will be a mile west on 16th Avenue, on the south side of the road.

Information: Contact Lake Superior State Forest, P.O. Box 798, Sault Ste. Marie, MI 49783; ☎ (906) 635-5281.

Algonquin Cross Country Ski Trail

Distance: 9 miles
Trail: Single track and two-track
Direction: Counter clockwise

The trail greets you with a fairly sandy two-track. Get used to the sand. Keep your eye peeled for the left-hand curve and steer along the bridge that takes you through a marsh. Just past the marsh is more sand and Post 2. Continue straight at the intersection for a little longer ride, reaching Post 3 at *Mile 1.3.* If there's been recent rain, this portion of the trail can be muddy, but beyond Post 3 you move onto a narrow two-track through mixed hardwoods with views of meadows and wetlands.

Post 4 is reached at *Mile 1.7*, just after crossing the Soo-Strongs Rail Trail. Head right at the junction and soon you pass a large wetlands, where you might hear a deer crashing about. A couple bridges provide some assistance over the particularly wet areas, and signs caution you to stay on the trail, which then meanders around the back of the wetlands. This area is somewhat sandy but does allow you to stop occasionally and check for signs of wildlife.

After some easy climbs Post 5 is reached at *Mile 2.7*. Here you have the option to continue on to post 6 or begin your return

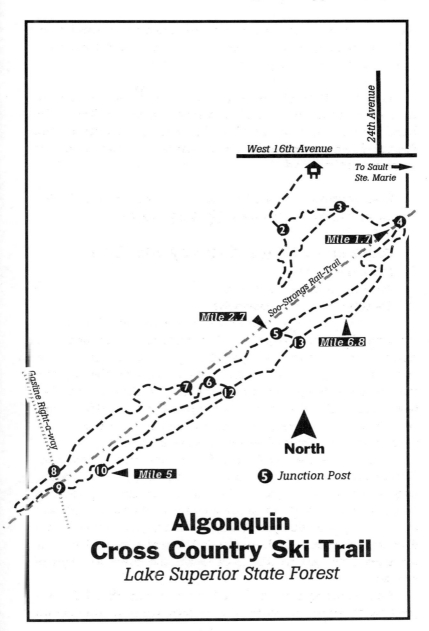

24th Avenue

West 16th Avenue

To Sault
Ste. Marie

Soo-Strongs Rail-Trail

Mile 1.7

Mile 2.7

Mile 6.8

Gasline Right-a-way

Mile 5

North

5 *Junction Post*

Algonquin
Cross Country Ski Trail
Lake Superior State Forest

51

by heading left to Post 13. At Post 7 you link up with an ORV trail, which is often chewed up and sandy. The trail continues to meander through a lowlands area and at time may force you to de-bike and walk around a puddle or two.

The next leg, to Post 8, is a rough ride. Partly because it appears ORV users prefer our trail to their own. If the bike trail is too chewed up for you, you may even want to ride theirs. At Post 8 the trail is lost in a gasline right-a-way which has apparently has become an ORV scramble area. To continue on the pathway, you have to cross this area and locate a white "No Snowmobiles" marker on the other side.

The most significant uphills so far are encountered just after **Mile 4**, or a half-mile before the pathway begins its return to the trailhead. Post 10 is reached at **Mile 5**. Veer right to stay on the outside loop and start out on a hard packed surface. On this leg to Post 12 you begin by skirting a ridgeline, forested on one side by pines, but within a half mile are back in a swampy area struggling through the loose surface of a rolling two-track. The sand can sap your strength, but hang in there.

After Post 13 the trail evens out and the riding gets easier. Once you reach Post 4 you backtrack much of the same route to the trailhead and parking area.

McNearney Ski Trail

County: Chippewa
Total Mileage: 9 miles
Terrain: Flat to rolling with several deep descents
Fees: None
Difficulty: Easy to moderate

McNearney is a classic U.P. ski trail, with the loops getting progressively more difficult the farther you are from the trailhead. The scenery also changes quickly. At one point you can be in lush, green bottomland and around the next bend you'll be cruising a ridgeline or in a meadow for a pleasant change of pace.

The system is composed of four loops that total 9 miles of mostly flat to rolling terrain. You can warm up on the Beginner's Loop west of the parking area, a mile of flat riding through mixed hardwoods. A quick spin around it will get your blood pumping and legs churning for the main route, a 6.3-mile ride of Camp 4, Big Pine and Forester's loops.

This can be a nice afternoon ride for anyone with a couple of free hours in Sault Ste. Marie, or part of a long weekend of riding. There are a number of other trails in the Soo area, including Algonquin Ski Trail and Pine Bowl Pathway.

Getting There: From Strongs on M-28, head north on Salt Point Road (also known as Strongs Road) just past the Strongs Motel. Within 5 miles national forest signs will point you toward the trail. Turn left into the trailhead.

Information: Contact the Sault Ste. Marie Ranger District, 4000 I-75 Business Spur, Sault Ste. Marie, MI 49783; ☎ (906) 635-5311.

McNearney Ski Trail

Distance: 6.3 miles
Trail: Single track and two-track
Direction: Counter clockwise

You begin near the cross-country ski warning shelter and enter a scrub forest. The trail is marked with blue diamonds, but it can be fairly overgrown here during the summer. The first hill, a gentle climb, pops up immediately and is followed by a few rollers. The trail at this point is a wide pathway.

Head right at the first intersection onto Camp 4 Loop and the second intersection is reached at **Mile 0.8.** Veer right here to continue on the Big Pine Loop and the perimeter of the trail system. Big Pine is a 2-mile loop rated *More Difficult* for skiers in the winter. You climb another gentle grade through a hardwood forest, often crunching over last fall's leaves. At **Mile 1.2** your effort is rewarded with a descent into a sweet-smelling stand of pine. The trail bottoms out and then immediately climbs again over the next ridge, descending into another stand of pine. After yet another climb you stay on the high trail for a bit, meandering along a ridgetop of aspen, oak and other hardwoods. Prudence is wise here, as there is a lot of deadfall, and inattention could cause a broken computer wire, spoke, or worse.

Traverse the meadow and the trail to your right will lead to Forester's Loop, the third and most challenging of the system. A post at **Mile 2.8** will direct you to turn right, but if you've had enough fun, veer left and head back to the parking lot.

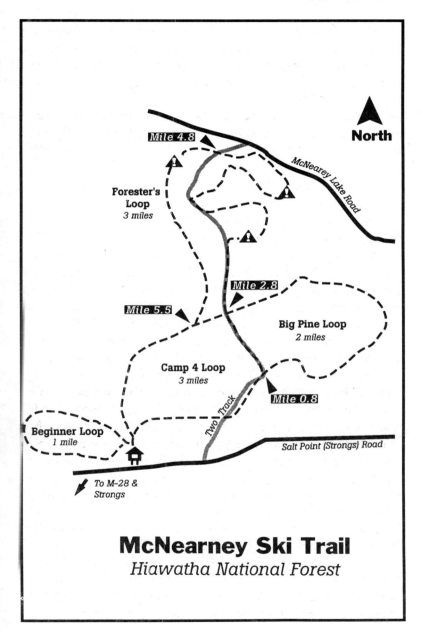

North

Mile 4.8

Forester's Loop
3 miles

McNearey Lake Road

Mile 2.8

Mile 5.5

Big Pine Loop
2 miles

Camp 4 Loop
3 miles

Mile 0.8

Beginner Loop
1 mile

Two Track

Salt Point (Strongs) Road

To M-28 &
Strongs

McNearney Ski Trail
Hiawatha National Forest

At the junction you move to two-track from single track and begin to pass Exclamation Point signs. Forester's Loop drops into a lush valley and then climbs out the other side. Be careful on this, and future, descents. The trail is rugged and pock-marked, and if you don't shift your weight and control your speed you could end up eating a mouthful of Upper Michigan's finest brown soil. I heard a lot of rather uncommon bird songs in this part of the trail, but you will have to stop to listen for them due to the crunching leaves. At *Mile 3.3* you'll come to another post and a two-track. Make a right back into the forest off the two-track just around a bend.

It's another downhill past a meadow and at ***Mile 3.7*** you veer to the right. Another pretty steep downhill is encountered and again remember to control your speed due to the earthen pot-holes. After another bend in the trail, you can see McNearney Lake Road on your right. You now are at the farthest point from the trailhead. The wildflowers seen here during early summer may help you rejuvenate and put a little extra spin in your pedals. This flat, mixed aspen and hardwood section of the trail helps you get your breath back as well.

At ***Mile 4.8*** Forester's Loop crosses the previously mentioned two-track. More rolling terrain is encountered, including a fast downhill with a large bump at the bottom. *Be careful or it can cause a crash.* A pair of meadows are a fresh change of pace from the hardwoods and from the far side of the second one you veer right. At ***Mile 5.3*** you chug up the steepest hill of the day, but it's rideable.

You'll wind around the top of another hill and then at ***Mile 5.5*** miles arrive at the junction with the Camp 4 Loop. The return to the parking lot is easy but you will hit some rollers and down-hills. These descents are nice and smooth, so now is the time to go all out. From here you'll roll through the entrance meadow and the trailhead reached at ***Mile 6.3***.

Canada Lakes Pathway

County: Luce
Total Mileage: 12 miles
Terrain: Flat to rolling forests with meadows and small lakes
Fees: Donation
Difficulty: Easy to moderate

At the turn of the century Newberry was a booming logging town where lumberjacks and river rats spent their hard-earned pay whooping it up on the weekends. Today it's the gateway to the most famous attraction in the Upper Peninsula, Tahquamenon Falls, and the loggers have long since been replaced by RVers in the summer and snowmobilers in the winter.

But mountain bikers touring the U.P. shouldn't pass up this town either. Newberry offers a wide range of accommodations and some the most affordable motel rates north of the Mackinac Bridge, a good restaurant in the Pickleman's Pantry and, best of all, a sweet little trail system in the Canada Lakes Pathway to work up an appetite.

Best known as a cross country ski trail and home of the Tahquamenon Falls Nordic Invitational, Canada Lakes can provide off-road cyclists a moderately easy but scenic ride with enough mileage for a good one or two-hour workout. The system totals

12 miles and features six loops of various lengths. The longest is the outside loop, which is 7.7 miles long, and contains the steepest hills of the area. For the most part the pathway is a wide single track with an occasional two-track segment.

Getting There: The pathway is 4 miles southeast of Newberry. From the junction of M-123 and M-28, head east one mile on M-28 and then south on County Road 403. Within 2 miles you'll reach the posted trailhead parking area.

Information: Contact the Lake Superior State Forest, P.O. Box 77, RR1, Newberry, MI 49868; ☎ (906) 293-5131.

Canada Lakes Pathway

Distance: 7.7 miles
Trail: Single track and two-track
Direction: Counter clockwise

At the trailhead there is a display board, vault toilets and a donation canister; please drop a few dollars in for upkeep of this pathway. To follow the outside loop numerically correct, you need to ride the route in a counter clockwise direction. The first half mile is along a flat two-track through a Depression-era forest, which then opens into a savannah and scrub forest after Post 2.

At Post 2 the trail begins to get a little more rugged and less worn. Post 3 is reached at **Mile 1** and here you plow through a prairie and fern meadow. The trail continues to get choppier, reaching Post 4 at **Mile 1.5** and Post 5 quickly after that. All intersections are clearly marked and feature posted maps.

At Post 5 you veer right to continue on the outside loop and for the first time enter a black diamond segment, which to skiers denotes a *Most Difficult* section. Near **Mile 2** there are some fairly significant rollers that provide a workout and a chance to coast for quite a ways into a mixed hardwood forest. Stay to the right at the next two "Y" intersections in the trail and continue to follow the blue pathway triangles to reach Post 6. Through the trees you

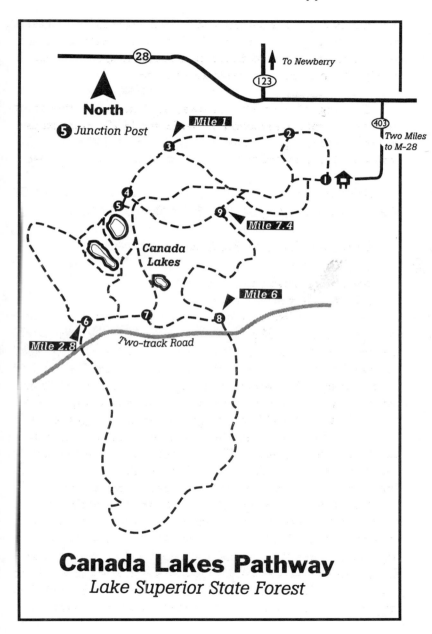

Canada Lakes Pathway
Lake Superior State Forest

should be able to get a glimpse of two of the three Canada Lakes while the trail to this point has been a combination of two-track, pathway and some dirt road.

After a significant climb, Post 6 is reached at the top of a hill at **Mile 2.8**, continue right to stay on the outside loop towards Post 8. This portion of the trail, a 3.5-mile segment, also is marked as *Most Difficult* by cross-country skiing authorities as it gets more rugged and overgrown. You endure some more rollers and bottomland, then cross a two-track road near **Mile 3** that is used for a nearby logging operation.

After riding through a young stand of hardwoods and an open meadow, a gentle but lengthy descent follows that offers a chance to catch your breath. Heads up at the bottom, where you have veer left into another open savannah, loosely sprinkled with pines. At **Mile 4.8** you'll find another directional arrow pointing you left toward Post 8. Continue around the bend, always veering left. The trail eventually changes back from a two-track to pathway. Admire the old-growth pines on the way through.

Just beyond **Mile 5** another intersection looms. Stay to the left, following the blue triangles. After a divine downhill run you arrive at a sign pointing to Post 8 in the next valley. Eventually the forest opens up and you meander through a pleasant stand of birch and then in 100 yards come to Post 8 at **Mile 6**.

The next mile or so is refreshingly rolly, and the forest thickens up with traditional U.P. flora, but flattens out just before **Mile 7**. You'll roll through Post 9 at **Mile 7.4** onto a well-defined two-track. Head right at the junction and continue straight to Post 1 at the trailhead parking area and your vehicle.

Seney National Wildlife Refuge

County: Schoolcraft
Total Mileage: 53 miles
Terrain: Flat, impoundments
Fees: None
Difficulty: Easy

What was once the wasteland that nobody wanted, today is one of the best places in Michigan to view wildlife while mountain biking. At 95,500 acres, Seney National Wildlife Refuge is the largest such refuge east of the Mississippi River.

The refuge surrounds the Great Manistique Swamp, which endured rough treatment beginning in the 1870s when loggers deliberately set fires to clear away the debris of a lumbering operation. A land development company then drained acre after acre of the swamp and sold the land to farmers in 1911. The farmers lasted about a year before discovering the soil would grow little and they had been swindled.

An environmental wasteland, Seney was deeded to the federal government during the Great Depression and rejuvenated by the Civilian Conservation Corps. CCC workers built dikes, dug ditches, and used other water-control devices to impound 7,000 acres of water in twenty-one major ponds that miraculously restored the marsh. More than 200 species of birds, including bald eagles and loons, can be spotted at the refuge as well as other wildlife ranging from deer and coyotes to otters and beavers.

You can view the wildlife from the refuge's interesting visitor center or by following its Marshland Wildlife Drive in your car. But the best way by far is on a mountain bike, following more than 50 miles of dikes and gravel roads that will lead you deep into the preserve.

The terrain is generally flat, the cycling extremely easy and the dikes and gravel roads well marked. This makes Seney ideal for beginners, families or others who enjoy stopping often to look for eagles, Canada geese, blue herons, egrets and loons in the various pools. Pack along a pair of compact binoculars for a better chance of spotting wildlife and plan on riding at dawn or dusk if you are really intent on seeing something wild.

Mountain bikes can be rented at Northland Outfitters (☎ 906-586-9801) in Germfask, which has put together a map of the five best rides for mountain bikers. The route described below is a combination of the Blue Loop and the Pink Loop for a 17.2-mile ride. Other loops are Blue (11 miles) and Orange (10.2 miles), Green (10.5 miles), which is the wildlife auto tour, and the Purple (4 miles), the refuge's fishing loop. The Green and Purple loops begin at the refuge's visitor center, all others from the Northern Hardwoods Cross Country Ski Area trailhead.

Germfask also has two good restaurants for a post-ride meal. The Wilderness Inn is a classic U.P. eatery, from the wood burning stove to the hot turkey sandwich that comes with a mountain of mashed potatoes in sea of gravy. The Eagle's Nest off M-77 on the north side of town is a little more upscale.

Getting There: The main entrance to the Seney National Wildlife Refuge and the visitor center is on the west side of M-77, just north of the small town of Germfask, or 10 miles from US-2. Most cycling routes, however, are picked up from the trailhead of Northern Hardwoods Cross Country Ski Area, which is south of Germfask at the end of Robinson Road.

Mountain biking opportunities at Seney National Wildlife Refuge include riding past a number of pools and impoundments where a variety of wildlife, especially birds and waterfowl, can be spotted.

Information: Contact Seney National Wildlife Refuge, HCR #2, Box 1, Seney, MI 49883; ☎ (906) 586-9851.

Pink Loop

Distance: 17.2 miles
Trail: Primarily gravel roads
Direction: Counter clockwise

The trailhead for the Northern Hardwoods Cross Country Ski Area is a small gravel parking lot where a gate prevents vehicles from continuing. Bypass the gate and follow the dirt road, staying to the left when it forks. Near **Mile 1** you skirt Upper Goose Pond on one side and smaller pond to the south and then cross a small bridge over Gray's Creek that flows between them.

At **Mile 2** you reach the junction with Pine Creek Road and the Pink Loop. Veer right on Pine Creek Road and stay right at the next immediate junction to remain on the gravel road heading north. For the next 2.5 miles you skirt Pine Creek then cross a cement bridge over the creek at **Mile 4.6**. Veer left at the junction on the other side to follow the two-track toward C-2 Pool.

At the beginning there's some hills and you'll need to shift, but the route quickly levels out to skirt the edge of the pool. You follow the south shore of C-2 for almost 3 miles. This is an excellent place to stop often and search for wildlife. Both loons and swans are often seen on the water, while just south of the pool near Sand Creek are a pair of nesting eagles.

At **Mile 8.2** you reach Driggs River Road. Veer left to head south and skirt the Driggs River for the next 2.5 miles. Just before **Mile 11** you turn left toward M-2 Pool. You'll encounter the largest hill of the ride here and then reach the impoundment. M-2's south shore is followed for the next 3 miles and halfway along you'll cross Sand Creek again. This is another good spot to search for waterfowl and loons.

You return to Pine Creek Road at **Mile 15**. Veer right and backtrack to the trailhead parking area.

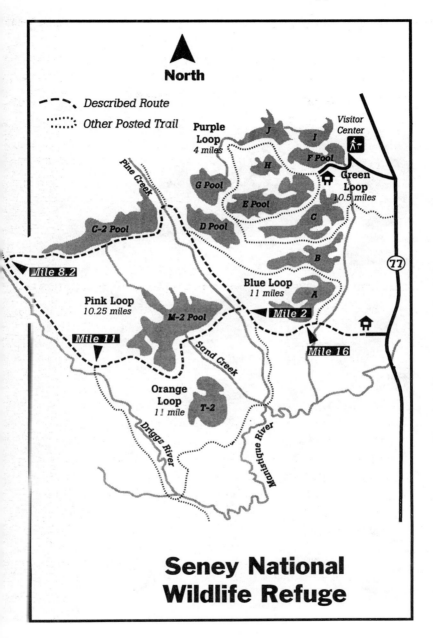

North

- – – Described Route
- ······· Other Posted Trail

Visitor Center

Purple Loop
4 miles

J   I

H   F Pool

G Pool

Green Loop
10.5 miles

E Pool

C-2 Pool

D Pool

C

Pine Creek

Mile 8.2

B

77

Pink Loop
10.25 miles

M-2 Pool

Blue Loop
11 miles

A

Mile 2

Mile 11

Sand Creek

Mile 16

Orange Loop
11 mile

T-2

Driggs River

Manistique River

Seney National Wildlife Refuge

Check Out Receipt

Independence Township Library (ITL)
243-625-2212
www.indelib.org
Monday, June 25, 2012 7:04:32 PM

41959

Item: 34633001493954
Title: Full tilt [sound recording]
Due   7/16/2012

Item: 34633001529922
Title: Dog-friendly New England : a traveler's companion
Due: 7/16/2012

Item   34633001226743
Title: Mountain biking Michigan : the 50 best trails and road routes in the Upper Peninsula
Due: 7/16/2012

Total Items: 3

Automated Phone Renewals 248-625-4633
Library website: http://www.indelib.org
LIBRARY HOURS:
MON-THURS 10AM-9PM
FRI 10AM-6PM
SAT 10AM-5PM
SUN CLOSED

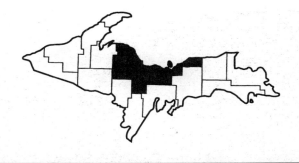

Munising

&

Marquette

A mountain biker walks over a log bridge along Bruno's Run , a trail in the Hiawatha National Forest.

Bruno's Run

County: Schoolcraft
Total Mileage: 9.7 miles
Terrain: Hills, lakes, Indian River, stands of old-growth hemlock
Fees: None
Difficulty: Moderate to strenuous

Although better known as a hiking trail, Bruno's Run is arguably the best all-around mountain biking trail in the Upper Peninsula. This trail has it all - satisfactory distance, climbs, swooping descents, mixed forest, vista views, lots of lakes, technical areas. You name it, this trail has it.

Part of the Hiawatha National Forest, Bruno's Run is located 13 miles south of Munising along H-13 and intersects McKeever Hills Ski Trail, another excellent run for mountain bikers. Between the two connecting systems off-road cyclists can enjoy almost 16 miles of trail through this lake-studded area.

There are some discrepancies about the length of Bruno's Run. The Munising Ranger District publishes a trail map that lists it as a 7.25-mile loop. But after carefully measuring it several times on a mountain bike, I put the ride at 9.7 miles, the distance used in this description.

Nearby are several national forest campgrounds, including Petes Lake, which Bruno's Run passes through. This rustic facility has 41 sites, including several walk-in sites, a picnic area and nice beach. Or extend your stay by booking a room in Munising and spending a day riding on Grand Island. Due to the popular Pictured Rock cruises that depart from Munising, there are a wide range of motels and cottages and other accommodations in the area.

Getting There: From M-28, east of the city of Munising, head south on H-13 for 11 miles. Trailheads for Bruno's Run are on H-13, opposite the entrance drive to Petes Lake, Petes Lake Campground and Widewaters Campground. There's limited parking available at each site.

Information: Contact the Munising Ranger District, RR2, P.O. Box 400, Munising, MI 49863; ☎ (906) 387-3700. For a complete list of lodging in the city call the Upper Peninsula Travel and Recreation Association at ☎ (800) 562-7134.

Bruno's Run

Distance: 9.7 miles
Trail: Single track
Direction: Counter clockwise

From the trailhead overlooking Moccasin Lake on H-13, head southwest to follow the trail in a counter clockwise direction. Within a third of a mile the trail veers to the left and climbs a steep hill, topping off on a ridge of hardwoods, pines and a view of Moccasin Lake.

You'll do some more climbing at **Mile 0.5** along a wider trail that ascends into a meadow sprinkled with wildflowers before climbing into more pines. The trail here, as it is through most of this ride, is a hard-packed single track. At **Mile 0.8** you'll come to an intersection with a snowmobile trail, but continue straight.

Eventually a sign appears, announcing that this portion of the trail was part of a rail line constructed by a lumber company in

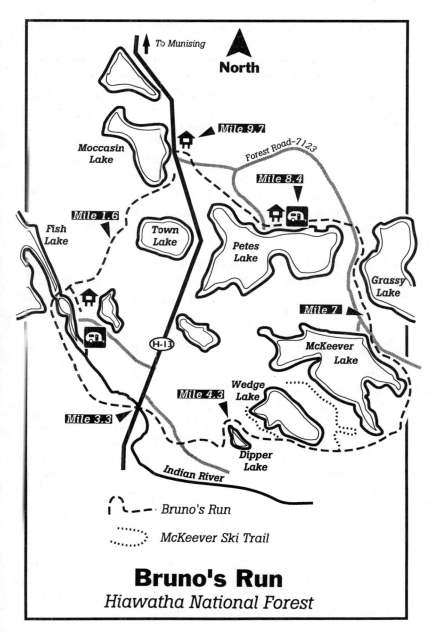

To Munising

North

Mile 9.7

Forest Road–7123

Mile 8.4

Moccasin
Lake

Mile 1.6

Fish
Lake

Town
Lake

Petes
Lake

Grassy
Lake

Mile 7

H-13

McKeever
Lake

Mile 4.3

Wedge
Lake

Mile 3.3

Dipper
Lake

Indian River

- - - Bruno's Run

······· McKeever Ski Trail

Bruno's Run
Hiawatha National Forest

1903. It's hard to believe railroad cars could fit through here. Make a left at the next arrow onto what appears to be a wider railroad grade, then veer to the right, following the blue diamonds. After about 150 feet veer right again back onto the single track.

The next half mile is a delight, with constant twisting and turning as the narrow trail weaves and circulates you over hills, ridgelines and ripples in the geography that require hardly any effort on your part. At **Mile 1.6** is the posted *Hemlock Cathedral*, where the pines tower above you. The trees are about halfway down a quarter-mile downhill where you can build your speed up in a hurry. But take time to pause in this cathedral with hemlock that foresters estimate to be 200 to 400 years old.

You'll pedal into a quick down-and-up with a bridge crossing in the middle, and another rather steep downhill with a couple of switchbacks thrown in for good measure. There are plenty of half-exposed tree roots here, so be careful. You cross a dirt road and then bottom out at **Mile 1.8** at a long bridge that traverses a channel connecting Fish Lake with the Widewaters portion of Indian River.

The next stretch is very scenic as the trail skirts Widewaters and then moves into a mature stand of pine. The trail is level here, making it a fast ride to where H-13 crosses the Indian River at **Mile 3.3**. Either splash your way across the river to the trail sign on the opposite bank, or if you want to keep your shoes dry, hike up to the highway bridge.

From H-13, skirt the river briefly and turn into the forest to do some more climbing before crossing FR-2258, a dirt road. More climbing follows until you top off at a bench at **Mile 4.3** with a great view of Dipper Lake below. This is just short of the halfway point in the ride and a great spot to take an extended break.

Beyond the bench the terrain develops a more definitive chop to it - up and down and up and down. After a lengthy downhill the trail merges into the posted C Loop of the McKeever Hills Trail at **Mile 5.2**. Veer right. More climbing, but another bench and over-

Bruno's Run includes skirting seven lakes and being able to stop at boat launches on McKeever Lake and Petes Lake .

look of a marshy meadow is your reward.

The trail here moves through a series of elongated whoop-de-doos, but without a lot of thigh-burning work on your part. A couple of downhills later at **Mile 6** is a stream from McKeever Lake flowing through a marshy hollow. Luckily, especially if it has been raining, piecemeal planking and a log bridge assist you in getting across. The shore of McKeever Lake is quickly reached and a nice breeze will chase away any bugs that followed you from the marsh. The next half mile is a lazy pedal along a wide pathway along the shoreline. At **Mile 6.8** the trail splits. Continue straight to reach a boat launch on McKeever Lake.

Bruno's Run veers to the right, crosses paved FR-2173 and at

Mile 7 arrives at a stream flowing into Grassy Lake. You'll soon get a closer look at the lake as the trail spits you down a fast little downhill chute. Remember that as you climb the significant uphill that follows. At the top you ride along a bluff overlooking the lake.

You break out at the Grassy Lake Overlook parking area at **Mile 7.6**, quickly return to the woods at the end of it and then recross FR-2173 at **Mile 8**. Look for the Bruno's Run bear sign and blue diamonds to re-enter the trail on the other side of the paved road.

You briefly follow a snowmobile trail, then veer left with the blue diamonds along a technical section The land is flat, but there are plenty of exposed, moss-covered tree roots and rocks to navigate around and over, and speed is impossible. Petes Lake Campground is reached at **Mile 8.4**, with the trail passing through the middle of it then into the day-use areas where there are picnic tables, vault toilets and a beach.

You re-enter the woods briefly before breaking out at the boat launch and then return to the woods again for the final stretch. At **Mile 9.5** you'll cross FR-2173 for a third time, and H-13 soon follows with the Moccasin Lake trailhead on the opposite side of the road.

McKeever Hills
Ski Trail

County: Alger
Total Mileage: 6.3 miles
Terrain: Flat to rolling forest with steep whoop-de-dos
Fees: None.
Difficulty: Easy to moderate

Although best known as a cross country ski trail, McKeever Hills is an itinerary-must for mountain bikers traveling through the central U.P. Part of the Hiawatha National Forest and managed by the Munising Ranger District, McKeever Hills is a 6.3-mile system of three loops with the B and more challenging C Loop making up the bulk of the mileage.

As a mountain bike destination, this is a very under-used gem, conveniently located in the middle of the Upper Peninsula. It's easy for anybody heading to Pictured Rocks, Marquette or even Escanaba to swing over to this segment of the Hiawatha National Forest for an hour or two of trail bliss. McKeever Hills offers something for every type of biker, whether you ride to enjoy scenic vistas and lake views or smile-provoking descents.

Want to spend all day here? It's easy to get a full day of riding by hopping from one trailhead to the another in this area. You can even ride McKeever Hills and Bruno's Run Trail without even getting off your bicycle.

Getting There: McKeever Hills is just south of Bruno's Run on H-13. From M-28 just east of Munising, head south on H-13 for 13 miles. The trailhead is across H-13 from Forest Glen Country Store.

Information: Contact the Munising Ranger District, RR2, P.O. Box 400, Munising, MI 49863; (906) 387-3700.

McKeever Hills Ski Trail

Distance: 6.8 miles
Trail: Single and two-track
Direction: Clockwise

The trail enters the woods on the east side of H-13 on what looks like a county road and then descends to a view of Pete's Lake on your left. Stay to the left at a "Y" intersection to pass up the short and flat A Loop and in 200 yards you'll arrive at a gate prohibiting motorized vehicles on the trail system. A half-mile from the gate is another "Y" intersection; continue straight for the B loop and the back portion of the trail. At *Mile 1* the ride becomes more rugged and rolly. You're now on a single track pathway.

Now you begin to work, but have a view of Pete's Lake on the left to ease the climbs. Trust me, the uphill work early in the ride pays big dividends later along the trail. At **Mile 1.3** you're rewarded with another view of the lake and then come to an intersection. Follow the directional arrow to the right. From here the trail becomes more topsy-turvy, and at **Mile 1.8** you arrive at Robert's Pond, which can be used to spot your location on a map.

The trail becomes more rough-cut and then passes a very scenic swamp and wetlands. A couple more elevation changes and you'll roll through a stand of towering pines that provide a natural cushion to the forest floor. From the towering pines the trail passes Ferrar Pond, which is connected to McKeever Lake. Did you pack along a rod and reel? If so, this may be a good place to wet a line.

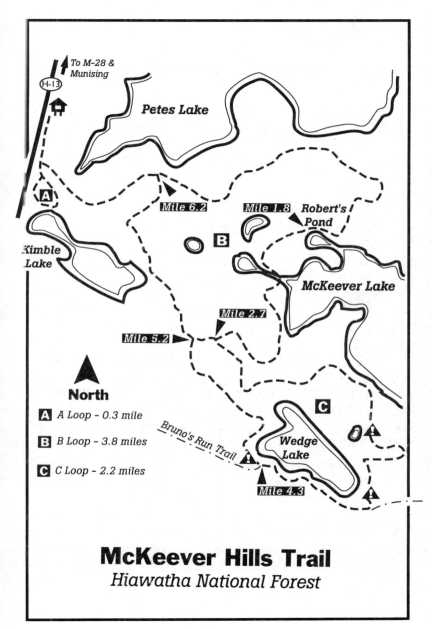

To M-28 &
Munising

H-13

Petes Lake

A

Mile 6.2

Mile 1.8

Robert's
Pond

B

Kimble
Lake

McKeever Lake

Mile 2.7

Mile 5.2

North

A *A Loop - 0.3 mile*

B *B Loop - 3.8 miles*

C *C Loop - 2.2 miles*

Bruno's Run Trail

C

Wedge
Lake

Mile 4.3

McKeever Hills Trail
Hiawatha National Forest

The Otter Slide is the first of several caution markers posted for cross country skiers. Why is it named Otter Slide? Otters like water, which you can clearly see at the bottom of the descent. The ground is sloppy here much of the summer but a log bridge has been erected for crossing the stream between the pond and lake. If you want to test your technical skills give it a shot. It's rideable, but the penalty for failure would be a nasty, wet fall.

At **Mile 2.3** an intersection appears; follow the trail path that bends to the right onto a rugged two-track road. Near a *McKeever Lake* sign are blue diamonds in the forest leading toward the lake but this route is for winter travel only and unrideable with mountain bikes. Stay on the two-track and climb. In less than a quarter mile is a spur to the right marked by a blue directional arrow. Take it.

The *Whoa!* caution sign signals your next standout downhill run. The trail is smooth and you can ride it hard to build up some speed and then use the momentum to carry you up the other side into some old-growth pines. At **Mile 2.7** is an intersection map. Here, you can either stay on the B loop or head onto the dizzying C Loop.

Congratulations for selecting the C Loop! Within a quarter mile into the C loop you'll see a brown sign indicating a stand of sugar maple trees. At this intersection, although it's not marked, head left. Travel past the two visitor parking signs and ignore the brown directional arrows (you're following blue ciamonds). At the next blue diamond make a right onto the dirt road. Go past a public access site for McKeever Lake and be prepared to enter more hilly terrain. Quick Silver arrives and if you've survived Whoa! you can take this run the same way. Enjoy the speed.

These whoop-de-dos are steep, so keep control of your bike. The Sinkhole descent turns at the bottom. In this portion of the trail you are either climbing or descending. Flat terrain is a thing of the past. At **Mile 3.8** you enter a forest of mixed hardwoods and ferns with a fairly open skyline. The trail quickly merges into Bruno's Run; steer to the right on single track.

At **Mile 4.3** the McKeever Hills Trail splits off and heads right. The C Loop retains some of the characteristics of Bruno's Run, however, as a tight single track. Closer to the lake the trail veers to the right, and you encounter the most extreme uphill of the ride. But your sweat-equity pays off on the backside with a sweet, fast descent into bottomland. Don't celebrate yet. The hill known as Thunder beckons, and it's an uphill battle. The next intersection is kind of funky, but head straight through it, following the blue diamonds.

After a quarter mile of leisurely pedaling down a two-track, a directional map pops up at **Mile 5.2**. Head left for the rest of B loop and the trailhead. This side of the B loop has gentle rollers with mixed forest and plenty of sun. There is one more significant downhill before you come to the intersection passed early in the ride. Head left to reach your vehicle in a little more than half a mile.

Most of the Valley Spur system is either wide trails or two-tracks through the hardwood forest just south of Munising.

Valley Spur Trail

County: Alger
Total Mileage: 26 miles
Terrain: Rolling hardwood forest
Fees: None
Difficulty: Easy to moderate

Valley Spur is one of four trail systems promoted by the Munising Ranger District of the Hiawatha National Forest for mountain biking. Of the four - Grand Island, Bruno's Run and Pine Marten Run - Valley Spur is the quickest and easiest to reach from Munising and M-28. This 26-mile trail system offers quality riding for novice riders while a segment of it, Loop 2, is technical enough for intermediate cyclists to test their skills and endurance.

Four loops have been posted with brown and white bicycle symbols and numbered at each junction and on location maps. Loop 1, a 12-mile route, is the easiest ride as most of it follows forest roads wide enough for two people to ride side-by-side. The highlight of this route is a short side trip to Truman Lake.

The other three loops follow existing ski trails and have been carefully chosen to keep bikers out of the low-lying wet areas that aren't a hinder to Nordic skiers in the winter. The route described below is a combination of Loop 3 and Loop 2, an 11.2-mile ride that offers the most hills and technical sections.

The Valley Spur day lodge, a beautiful log building, is closed after ski season but during the rest of the year you'll find vault toilets, drinking water and a large display map at the main trailhead off M-94. There is also a second trailhead for mountain bikers, off Forest Road 2264, a half mile east of M-94. This provides easy access to the flatter sections of the system, particularly Loop 4.

Getting There: From Munising, head south on M-28 and within a mile turn west M-94. The main trailhead is reached within 5 miles and is well posted along M-94.

Information: Contact Munising Ranger District, Munising, MI 49862; ☎ (906) 387-2512.

Valley Spur Trail

Distance: 11.2 miles
Trail: Mostly two-tracks with some single track segments
Direction: Counter clockwise

To ride the perimeter of Loops 2 and 3, it's best to begin on Loop 3 and follow it in a counter clockwise direction. This will allow you to follow Loop 2, the most difficult section, in the direction marked on some trail maps.

Practically next to the day lodge is a three-way intersection. Begin by heading south on the trail to the far right, which parallels M-94 and is marked as Loop 1 and Loop 3. The first half mile is a moderate climb along a two-track into mixed hardwoods and a sprinkling of birch. For being so close to the trailhead this is a scenic part of the system with hills rising on both sides of you.

At **Mile 1** is the intersection where Loop 4 splits off to the left. Continue straight for the peripheral loop. A half mile later is an intersection with a ski trail. Head straight through that as well, following the brown and white bicycle symbols.

The trail continues as a two-track, ideal for riding two-abreast, and flattens out as you move into a stand of pine. The next posted intersection is reached at **Mile 2**. Head left to pedal into the interior of the trail system and remain on Loop 3. Loop 1, a flat, lengthy trip along mostly dirt forest roads, heads straight.

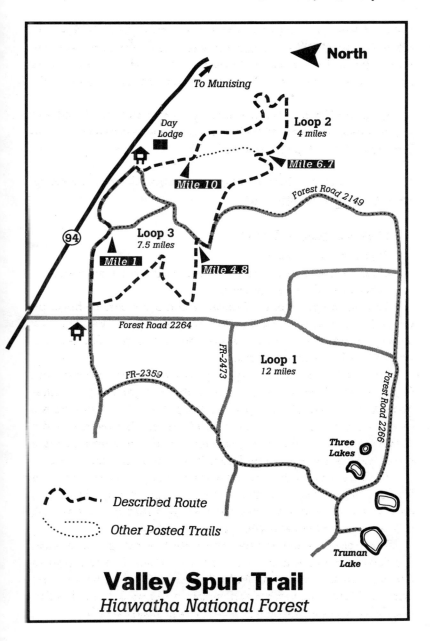

At **Mile 2.4** the trail passes the remnants of an old logging operation, including what appears to be a loading area for trucks. Continue straight and at **Mile 3.2** you'll have to make a sharp right to stay on the two-track trail. Be aware there are lots of ski markers on this system, but the numerous brown and white bicycle symbols, posted about every quarter mile, should keep you on the right route.

Another major intersection is reached at **Mile 4**. Veer left onto a dirt road and in less than a mile you'll reach where Loop 4 and Loop 1 split off to the left, the way to go if you've had enough. This ride continues along the middle trail and makes a gentle climb to a post at **Mile 5.7**.

The trail continues to be an easy pedal over flat terrain until you pass the entrance of The Pinery, a cross country ski trail. The mountain bike route heads straight into a downhill that's steep, fast and smooth - but grab a handful of brake at the bottom, as you have to make a hairpin right turn into Loop 2 at **Mile 6.7**.

The terrain along Loop 2 changes in a hurry to hills and the next downhill, another fast, smooth gem. At **Mile 7** you climb a grinding, wide single track. Gone are the monotonous segments of Loop 3. Here the trail narrows to rolling single track that at best is minimal and overgrown. A half-mile long downhill allows you to get your speed up, but stay in control, there's a lot of turns ahead. The downhill ends in a lush bottomland, where its time to pay the piper with an immediate climb. In mountain biking you take, you give. After the climb you skirt a ridge along a narrow single track with brush hitting both legs. Another series of downhills take you down the side of the ridge.

From here you will spin over a series of down-and-ups; it's either up or down on this segment. There are several Caution markers for skiers, but I found the trail to be very smooth. At **Mile 9.6** miles is an intersection. The bike route follows the natural flow to the left and emerges onto a two-track. A third of a mile later you'll hit the end of Loop 2. From here, make a right to reach the parking lot in less than a mile at the end of Loop 3.

Grand Island

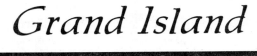

County: Alger
Total Mileage: 38 miles
Terrain: Cliffs overlooking
Lake Superior, beaches,
rolling forests
Fees: Ferry passage from Munising
Difficulty: Moderate

When people talk of Grand Island they talk about the views. There are so many panoramas along the peripheral trail on this 13,000-acre island, you soon lose count. There are spots on this national forest recreation area where it's possible to stand on the edge of a 200-foot sandstone cliff and gaze upon the endless sea that is Lake Superior or marvel at the sculptured beauty of the famed Pictured Rocks on the horizon.

Although this is one of the longest mountain bike rides described in this guide, it is still an adventure within the grasp of most intermediate off-road cyclists. The key is allowing yourself plenty of time to enjoy the ride and the views without having to rush at the end of the day to make the last ferry. And you don't want to miss that ferry. This is, after all, an island without any services or facilities other than a few rustic campsites.

On the other hand, if you do pack along camping equipment,

you can spend a night or two at the sites on Murray Bay or Trout Bay beaches and then take your time exploring the island. Whether you spend the night or not, carry a bottle of insect repellent when biking Grand Island any time in the summer. If you're planning to be there during the Upper Peninsula's notorious black fly season, from mid-May to mid-June, even a head net is not being too extreme. The other important item to carry is drinking water. At this time there is no source of safe water on the island so either have a quart or two with you or a filter to treat surface water.

Grand Island is an experimental multiple-use recreation area for the Hiawatha National Forest. There are more than 30 miles of roads and trails and a portion of them are open to cars and trucks throughout the summer. Off-road vehicles are also allowed on some bike trails from October through December so hunters can access areas during the Michigan deer season.

But during the summer a majority of the trails are open only to mountain bikes and hikers. This route not only follows the perimeter of the island for the best views but stays mostly on trails designated for foot-and-bicycle travel only.

Getting There: Grand Island Ferry Service provides transport to Grand Island daily during the summer from a dock just west of Munising off M-28. Ferries depart Munising at 9 a.m., noon, 3:30 p.m. and 6:30 p.m. For more information or prices call the company at ☎ (906) 387-3503.

Information: Contact the Munising Ranger District, 400 Munising Dr., Munising, MI 49862; ☎ (906) 387-3700.

Grand Island National Recreation Area
Distance: 22 miles
Trail: Single track, two-track and dirt roads
Direction: Clockwise
The trail begins at Williams Landing, where the ferry docks. A directional map just beyond the wharf will point you left (west) to

A mountain bike trip to Grand Island begins and ends with passage on a ferry for the short run from Munising to the Lake Superior island.

ride the peripheral island trail in a clockwise direction. This part of the trail is a wide single track through mixed hardwoods and pines. Near **Mile 1** you're rewarded with the first scenic view of Lake Superior along a shoreline that presents an excellent opportunity for rockhounds. But don't get too sidetracked looking for agates and greenstones, there is a long ride ahead of you.

At **Mile 2** views of the shoreline cliffs appear to the north and it's exciting to know you will be there shortly. The terrain has been flat up to this point and forested with stands of grandfatherly pines. A half-mile later the trail becomes more rocky as it begins a gentle climb. Sporadic gaps in the treeline facing Lake Superior let you keep track of your elevation gain.

At **Mile 3** the trail begins to veer inland through the thick forest and within a mile passes the first of a handful of private residences. Please respect the dwellings and the privacy of the families who own them. Blue trail markers will lead you around the residences and onto a steady, but not steep, climb that lasts for almost a mile.

At this point the trail narrows to a single track while gaps in the mature hardwoods let you gaze at the shoreline bluffs for an idea of how high you've climbed. It's pretty high. Eventually you're riding along the edge of the cliffs and the views are awesome. Past **Mile 6** the climbs becomes fairly steep, but the trail is very grippy and easy to spin up.

Payback for that sweaty uphill is rewarded at **Mile 7** with a descent that contains several wooden steps. *Be extremely careful here!* You are literally on the edge of a cliff where a loss of balance could result in a long fall. This descent continues for the next mile on a sweet single track. At **Mile 8** there is a great spot for a break as the forest opens up for a wide-angle view of the cliffs in the northwest corner of the island. You can rest your wrists here from all the braking. Another great view is reached within a mile after you pass some scrub forest and a savannah.

At **Mile 10.5** is the northern tip of Grand Island, and located here is a junction with a road cutting through the interior of the island. Open to vehicles, this road could be used to reach Williams Landing within 10 miles if you've had enough single track for the day. At **Mile 11** is a high suspended bridge across a gorge, providing passage to the eastern half of the island. This is a great place for pictures documenting your adventure. There's also a little-used beach nearby, enticing you to cool off or dip into your backpack for lunch.

A second posted junction is reached at **Mile 11.4** with an overgrown trail heading right into the interior of the island. This ride stays on the peripheral trail because I'm a sucker for scenery. A mile later a clearing in the treeline reveals a unique cave carved out at water's edge. This is the last view for at least a mile as the trail meanders inland briefly through a rolling forest. At **Mile 13.8** you return to the shoreline and the trail continues as a single track, offering up some nice downhills.

At **Mile 16.6** is another posted map, marking the southern

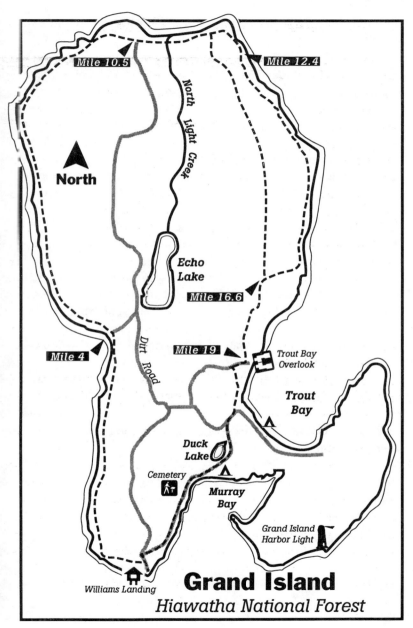

Mile 10.5

Mile 12.4

North
Light
Creek

North

Echo
Lake

Mile 16.6

Mile 4

Mile 19

Dirt Road

Trout Bay
Overlook

**Trout
Bay**

**Duck
Lake**

Cemetery

**Murray
Bay**

Grand Island
Harbor Light

Williams Landing

Grand Island
Hiawatha National Forest

junction of that overgrown trail. Continue south and in another mile the trail widens to a two-track. It was along this stretch that I found some very fresh bear scat on the trail, a reminder that the island's wildlife includes black bears. A view of Munising Bay, Miner's Castle, and Miner's Beach pops up at Trout Bay Overlook.

You veer right onto a vehicle two-track briefly at **Mile 18.2** and then head left to continue south on a tight single track through a thick forest. It's all downhill for the first half mile, where you need to keep an eye peeled for rocks.

At **Mile 19** is a post where you veer right onto another vehicle dirt road. You'll quickly reach a fork in the road; veer left here to continue south toward Duck Lake. The small lake soon appears in the middle of a stand of pine before you begin descending toward it, passing vault toilets and the Murray Bay campsites within a mile.

Take a time out to check the cemetery passed on the right. Family members of Abraham H. Williams, the first white settler to homestead the island, are buried here, some dating back to 1854. An interesting historical sign details life on the island in early 1800s, including how the Williams family occasionally found drowned sailors washed up on shore.

The next mile is a dirt road that takes you past more cottages of islanders, who will wave a hello if they see you. At **Mile 21.7** this road ends at a junction with the interior road to Echo Lake. Make a left here and in a third of a mile you'll be back at Williams Landing waiting for the ferry.

Anderson Lake Pathway

County: Marquette
Total Mileage: 6 miles
Terrain: Hilly hardwood and pine forests
Fees: None
Difficulty: Easy to moderate

Anderson Lake Pathway is four and half miles of fun. Located in the Escanaba River State Forest, a half hour south of Marquette, the pathway is more descents than climbs and a place where you can let it all hang out on the relatively safe downhills.

It's also a scenic area. The trails roll through a hilly terrain and past pines, stands of hardwoods, wet areas that keep you honest and three small lakes. Nearby is Anderson Lake and on its west shore is a very pleasant state forest campground of 19 rustic sites and a good swimming area where you can cool off after the ride.

The pathway is a system of three loops that total more than 6 miles. This ride follows the 4.5-mile outside loop but shorter outings of 3.5 miles or 2.5 miles are possible. Built primarily for cross country skiing, you'll find the trail generally wide in most places. There are some stretches of technical single track, however, ideal for beginners and intermediate bikers wishing to test newly acquired off-road skills.

Getting There: From either US-41 near Marquette or US-2 from Gladstone take M-35 to Gwinn. West of the small town, turn left on Serenity Drive and head south to the first stop sign, County Road 557. Head south two miles to the Anderson Lake Campground entrance. The trailhead is at the entrance of the campground, at Post 1. Or you can skip the paved road by entering the campground and parking near the Post 3, close to the self-registration area.

Information: Contact Escanaba River State Forest, 6833 US-2, US-41 and M-35, Gladstone, MI 49837; ☎ (906) 474-6442.

Anderson Lake Pathway

Distance: 4.5 miles
Trail: Wide single track
Direction: Clockwise

From the campground registration area head left on the trail, at this point a wide single track, toward Post 4. The pine forest here is very nice, with old growth trees and a carpet of soft needles and moss. At **Mile 0.8** you'll reach an intersection with one spur heading right toward a hiker's only interpretive trail around Flack Lakes. Mountain bikers need to continue straight toward Post 4 just ahead. The trail climbs to Post 5 through a healthy mix of hardwoods, including, birch, oak, maple, and aspen.

At the Post 5 junction you head southwest and can build some speed on a nice little descent at **Mile 1** just before reaching Post 6. Here the trail crosses a two-track and heads due south to meander through some subtle yet pleasing geographical changes. The forest alternates from old-growth pine and birch to young scrub. From here the trail opens up and starts getting more hilly at **Mile 1.4** as it swings north toward Post 7.

In the next half mile you descend twice into some soggy bottomland, the second time is a particularly wet section where a hand-built bridge will help you out. Motor through it if you can but be prepared to endure wet shoes when you pedal out the

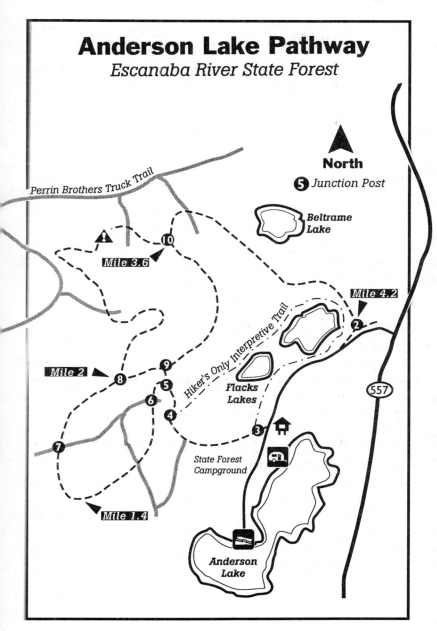

Anderson Lake Pathway
Escanaba River State Forest

North

5 *Junction Post*

Perrin Brothers Truck Trail

Beltrame Lake

Mile 3.6

10

1

Mile 4.2

Mile 2

2

Hiker's Only Interpretive Trail

9

8

5

6

Flacks Lakes

557

4

7

3

State Forest Campground

Mile 1.4

Anderson Lake

other side. Post 8 is reached at **Mile 2**, steer left to continue on to the third loop, Post 10, and the most difficult portion of the trail.

After some prolonged climbing through mostly evergreen and birch stands you'll follow a ridgeline and then climb some more before the forests changes to mostly hardwoods, lots of trailside ferns, and plenty of deadfall to navigate around. At **Mile 2.6** you'll grin all the way down a sweet little downhill single track through a narrow - and I mean narrow - chute in the forested hillside. That stretch is great, but there is a bill to pay, as you will find out after crossing the adjoining bottomlands and face the ensuing climb. Once at the top of the next hill there are two ways to descend, the *more difficult* and the *most difficult*. I recommend the most difficult but both runs are smooth and meet at the bottom of the hill under towering pine trees.

You'll enjoy another descent, a barely noticeable climb, then another, longer downhill. At **Mile 3.6** is the Post 10, and you veer left. The forest here is mixed evergreen and hardwoods, with an abundance of ferns growing on either side of the trail. At **Mile 4.2** you reach Post 2 post near the campground entrance road. Head right on the road to reach Post 3 and your vehicle in a quarter mile.

Blueberry Ridge Pathway

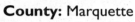

County: Marquette
Total Mileage: 15 miles
Terrain: Rolling forest with considerable sand
Fees: Donations
Suggested riders: Moderate

As a cross country ski trail, Blueberry Ridge Pathway is renown. Home of the Red Earth Loppet every March and the training site for the Northern Michigan University ski teams, the 15-mile system is often regarded as the finest Nordic area in the Upper Peninsula if not the entire state.

As a mountain bike destination, Blueberry Ridge is mediocre at best due to the heavy amounts of sand that are encountered on the trails. Still, if you're in the Marquette area for a spell it's another place to ride if you have already tackled Harlow Lake, Range Mountain Bike Area and Anderson Lake Pathway. The sand can be a pain at times, but the forest is interesting and the trail system a short trip no matter where you're staying in the city.

The trail system is composed of seven loops with the northern ones, Crossroads and Husky loops in particular, being generally flat easy routes. It's the southern loops that contain the most hills and steepest slopes. This 13-mile ride is the outside perimeter of the pathway, which includes portions of all the loops.

Getting There: The trail system is 6 miles from Marquette and serviced by two trailheads. The main trailhead is located off Country Road 553, just south of its intersection with County Road 480.

Information: Contact DNR Field Office, P.O. Box 632, Teal Lake Rd., Ishpeming, MI 49849; ☎ (906) 485-1031.

Blueberry Ridge Pathway

Distance: 13 miles
Trail: Single track and two-track
Direction: Clockwise

From the trailhead off CR-553, follow a two-track into the forest that turns into a trail before reaching Post 2, the start of the Husky Loop. Stay to the left to follow the peripheral route. You will hear the traffic from this segment but just past **Mile 1** enter a rolling topography and within a half mile come to your first steep climb of the day.

Equally steep downhills are encountered as you follow the Spartan Loop, a segment that is sandy but rideable. You'll hit some major sand traps just past Post 4 at **Mile 2** and then face a significant climb within a third of a mile. A few turns later the trail turns into as a newly-built fire road with another tough uphill. But take heart, at the top of this climb you are treated to some reciprocation in the ensuing downhill.

The terrain becomes rolling again as you head for Post 5 and then continue south for Post 6, reached at **Mile 4.7**. Here you swing north for Post 7 and within a quarter mile face a steep downhill run with a bypass to the side. Post 7 is reached at **Mile 5.6**. The trail swings left here to enter the Superior Loop. You pass through a refreshing stand of aspen trees and then merge into a newly-cut two-track that can be pretty soft and strength-sapping.

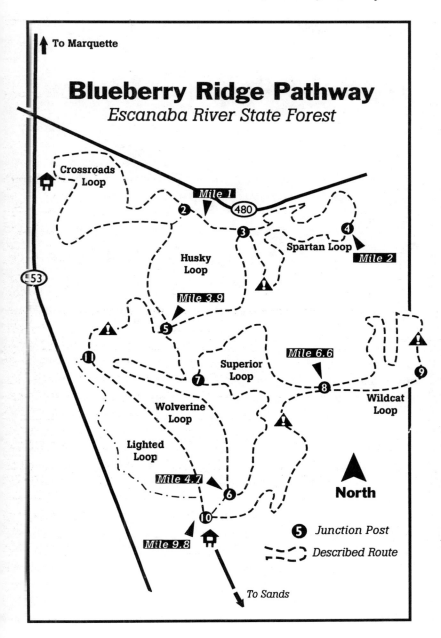

One of the many steep hills that are encountered along the Blueberry Ridge Pathway, a noted ski trail just south of Marquette.

The Wildcat Loop, a black diamond segment for skiers, is reached at Post 8 at **Mile 6.6**. This loop is 1.7 miles long and less maintained than the other loops, making for a refreshing change. But you need to be alert for deadfall and be prepared to navigate around trail bumps.

The trail remains hilly as you return to Post 8 and continue with the rest of the Superior Loop, again a two-track of very loose soil. At **Mile 7** you're rewarded with a drawn-out, high-speed downhill. Keep that in mind as you prepare to granny-gear it up the next incline.

Post 10 is reached near **Mile 9.8**. Turn right toward the light posts. This segment of the Lighted Loop is one long straightway where its possible to build up some speed to Post 11. On the other side of the junction you enjoy a nice long downhill, bottoming out on the Husky Loop. From here it's a short ride back to Post 2, the first intersection of the day. Turn left and the parking lot is less than a mile away.

Harlow Lake Pathway

County: Marquette
Total Mileage: 6.2 miles
Terrain: Wooded rolling hills and a steep uphill
Fees: None
Difficulty: Moderate

Just 5 miles northwest of Marquette on County Road 550 is Little Presque Isle State Forest Recreation Area, an incredibly scenic bit of wild country that includes Sugar Loaf Mountain, Hogback Mountain and 4 miles of pristine Lake Superior shoreline. Situated in the middle of this a 3,040-acre tract is the Harlow Lake Pathway, a cross country ski trail now open to mountain bikers.

This 6-mile trail system is a surprisingly sweet little ride, the first place most locals head to when they want to do a little off-road biking. It's rated as a moderate outing only because of some obstructions on the trail - large U.P. style rocks, roots and branches - and not because it's a technical single track.

There's not a lot of twists and turns but sometimes it's difficult to stay on course as the trail is not well-marked. Only sporadic intersection markers and a few location maps have been posted along the system. Hopefully that will change in the future;

meanwhile, the trail is fairly well-cut and easy to follow once you get into it.

Getting There: From Marquette, head north on County Road 550 toward Big Bay. Within 5 miles the county road passes the large Sugar Loaf sign, marking the trailhead to this popular peak, and then the posted trailhead for Wetmore Pond, a short interpretive trail on the west side of the road. In less than a mile from Sugar Loaf is a yellow gate on the west side of the road, marking the entrance of Clark's Gravel Pit, an abandoned pit. You can park by the yellow gate.

Information: Contact Escanaba River State Forest, 1985 U.S. 41 West, Ishpeming, MI 49849; ☎ (906) 485-1031.

Harlow Lake Pathway

Distance: 6.2 miles
Trail: Single track and dirt roads
Direction: Counter clockwise

From Clark's Gravel Pit follow the trail to the right to quickly enter the woods. Immediately you're immersed in a stand of birch trees, hardwoods and evergreens along a trail that starts out flat and easy as a mixture of single track and wide paths. What's nice about this trail is that you hit no significant uphills before enjoying a sweet descent.

After crossing Potluck Creek, veer right at the junction. At **Mile 1.5** you reach a state forest rental cabin, one of six located around Harlow Lake, and then come to Post 2. Views of the 64-acre lake are enjoyed along this stretch but be careful as the ground can be sloppy if there's been recent rain. Just before **Mile 2** you make a left across a railroad grade and then Harlow Lake Road to continue on to Post 3.

In the next mile the trail widens and leads you up a gentle but sustained climb, making you pay the price for that beautiful lake scenery you just enjoyed. Post 3 is along a dirt road and reached

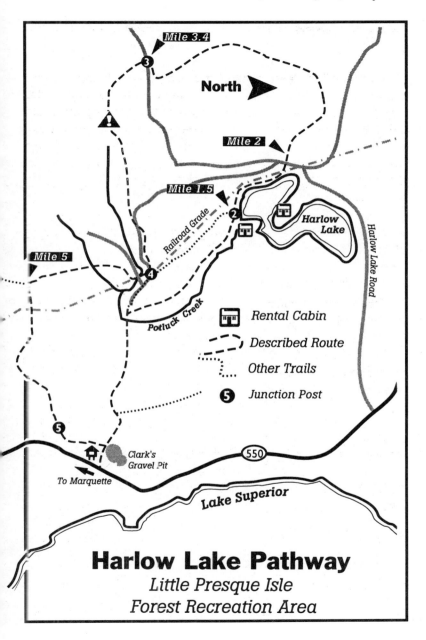

North

Mile 3.4

Mile 2

Mile 1.5

Mile 5

Railroad Grade

Harlow Lake

Harlow Lake Road

Potluck Creek

Rental Cabin

Described Route

Other Trails

5 Junction Post

Clark's Gravel Pit

550

To Marquette

Lake Superior

Harlow Lake Pathway
Little Presque Isle
Forest Recreation Area

A young mountain biker pauses for a rest while following the Harlow Lake Pathway, a favorite for Marquette residents.

at **Mile 3.4**. On the other side of the road the trail returns to a single track and climbs steeply uphill for the next third of a mile.

If you don't like climbing, just keep concentrating on the up-coming descent - the uphill effort is worth it. For more than a mile you get to enjoy an awesome, two-stage downhill run. Half-way through the run you'll veer right onto a fire road for about 350 feet then a left back onto the trail to enjoy the rest of the descent. The forest here is wonderful, but it's hard to notice because your momentum will blur the trees as you concentrate on the narrow path.

You bottom out at Post 4 at **Mile 4.6** in a pine forest. Here the trail swings south as a rugged single track. For an easier ride you can head down the railroad grade instead, intersecting the trail in a half mile. Either way turn left (east) at the next trail junction, reached at **Mile 5**, and follow the return arrow toward Post 5.

Time now for a change of scenery and trail surface. The last leg of the ride includes a rocky descent with a sharp turn built in. Many cyclists end up walking parts of this stretch and taking the time to enjoy the terrain with its stone outcroppings. Others see this last segment to the parking lot as an excellent test of their mountain biking skills. Either way be especially careful here.

The trail will take you back to Clark's Gravel Pit and the parking lot off County Road 550.

The scenery in the Range Mountain Area Trail System includes a pair of ski jumps, including this 90-meter ramp, in an area called Suicide Bowl.

Range
Mountain Bike Trails

County: Marquette
Total Distance: 25 miles
Terrain: A variety of terrain including wooded ridges with rapid elevation changes and lakes
Fees: Trail pass
Difficulty: Easy to strenuous

In 1997, local cyclists from Ishpeming and the surrounding area formed the Range Mountain Bike Association to designate, maintain and promote a trail system in their region. By the end of the year more than 25 miles of trails had been identified with a good portion of them posted and mapped.

The goal of the association is to develop the Suicide Bowl and Hill Street cross country ski trails as a mountain bike area. This rugged area of ridges and lakes south of Ishpeming, home of the Suicide Bowl ski jumps, would then be linked with the trail system at Al Quaal Park, north of town, by the Partridge Creek Trail and the Jasper Ridge Trail. Departing north from Al Quaal would be the Teal Lake Trail and the Deer Lake Trail into an undeveloped, wilderness-like area.

When completed, Range Mountain will be one of the most

extensive mountain biking areas in the Upper Feninsula with a wide variety of terrain, including steep ridges, isolated lakes, rocky bluffs with spectacular vistas and those famous ski jumps. In the middle of the system is the Jasper Ridge Brewery, the perfect place to end any afternoon on the trails.

Presently the Hill Street Trails, Al Quaal Park and Jasper Ridge Trail are posted and easy to follow. Described below is the Hill Street system, while Al Quaal is covered as the next ride of this book. The trailhead for the Jasper Ridge Trail is located behind the Jasper Ridge Brewery, just off US-41/M-28, behind the Best Western Country Inn.

If you're contemplating riding the Range Mountain Trail System, stop at the Ishpeming-Negaunee Area Chamber of Commerce (☎ 906-486-4841) on US-41/M-28 as you enter Ishpeming from the east. The office is open Monday through Friday from 8 a.m. to 5 p.m. and will have the latest maps and information on how well portions of the system are marked. This is particularly important with the Suicide Bowl trails, which in 1997 were very difficult to follow. Eventually a trail fee will be instituted to help pay for the maintenance of the system.

Getting There: To reach the trailhead for Hill Street Trails from US-41/M-28 head south on Third Street at the U.S. National Ski Hall of Fame. When Third Street ends at the high school, turn left at Pearl Street, right on Fourth Street and left on Division Street. Within a block veer right on Jasper Street and then veer right again on Hill Street. The trailhead and parking area is at the end of Hill Street.

To reach Suicide Bowl, stay on Division Street and continue east. Just beyond the city limits of Negaunee is the posted entrance to Suicide Bowl.

Information: Contact Ishpeming-Negaunee Area Chamber of Commerce, 661 Palms Ave., Ishpeming, MI 49849; ☎ (906) 486-4841.

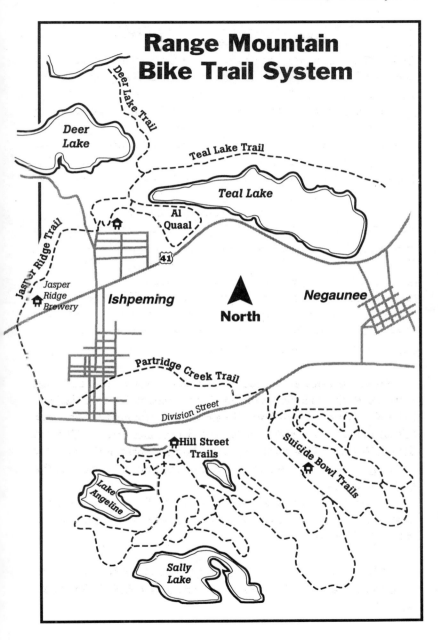

Range Mountain Bike Trail System

Hill Street Trails

Distance: 5 miles
Trail: Single track and two-track
Direction: Counter clockwise

By the fall of 1997, Hill Street Trails (also referred to as Cleveland Trails) were well posted with white mountain biker symbols and easy to follow. The following route is a 5-mile ride that includes the spectacular Lookout Loop along with the Tilden Trail for a ride that is rated moderate.

For an easier ride, bypass the Tilden Trail, which will shorten the route to a 4-mile loop. To lengthen your ride or to make it more challenging, add Sandi's Trail or Minnie's Loop. By including both of them you will end up with a 7-mile loop that will be a challenging ride recommended for advanced bikers.

From the parking lot at the end of Hill Street, walk around the locked gate and begin riding on the wide single track beyond it. The surface here and throughout much of the system is hard packed but very rocky. White mountain biker symbols will lead you up a hill and then right at a junction for Lookout Loop. Skirting a bluff, you arrive at a posted *Scenic Overlook* spur within a half mile. The short spur leads to a rocky bluff with a panoramic view of Lake Angeline and a cluster of houses on its west shore.

Back on the main trail you quickly arrive at a second *Scenic Overlook.* This spur is slightly longer but ends with a better view of Lake Angeline. The main trail makes a short climb from the second lookout, sidles an intriguing rock bluff then begins a rapid descent. At **Mile 1.2** a junction with a trail map pops up with South Cedar Trail and Lizard Loop heading left.

Veer right to stay on the main trail. A gentle descent to a powerline follows. The trail goes under the electrical wires (though the tendency here is to follow the powerline trail) and then throws a steep downhill segment at you before bottoming out in a meadow and crossing a second powerline.

A stiff climb follows to the posted junction of Sandi's Trail, reached at **Mile 1.8**. This 1.5-mile loop veers to the right

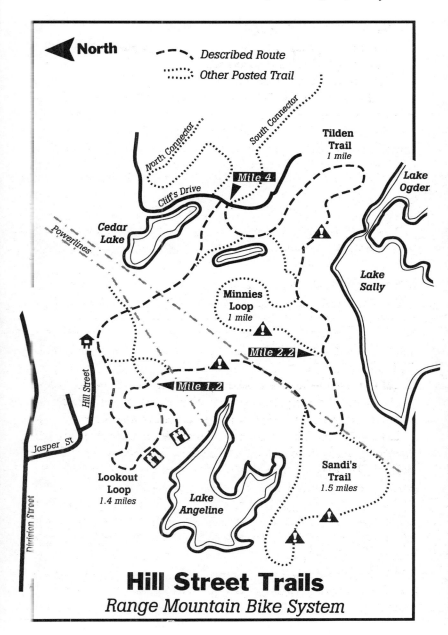

North

- - - ➤ *Described Route*
·····: *Other Posted Trail*

North Connector

South Connector

Tilden Trail
1 mile

Cliff's Drive

Mile 4

Lake Ogder

Powerlines

Cedar Lake

Lake Sally

Minnies Loop
1 mile

Mile 2.2

Mile 1.2

Hill Street

Jasper St

Lookout Loop
1.4 miles

Lake Angeline

Sandi's Trail
1.5 miles

Division Street

Hill Street Trails
Range Mountain Bike System

A mountain biker crosses a old iron and wood bridge while riding in the Hill Street Trails, part of the Range Mountain Bike Trail System.

along a two-track and is the most challenging segment of the Hill Street system with two long climbs followed by gonzo downhill runs.

The main trail veers left as a two-track and continues climbing, reaching the return of Sandi's Trail within a quarter mile. You then enjoy a gentle downhill run to the junction with Minnie's Loop, reached at **Mile 2.2**. This mile-long loop is also rated as a challenging segment though it is not as difficult as Sandi's Trail.

The main trail veers right, quickly passes the return of Minnies Loop and then at **Mile 2.6** arrives at the junction with the Tilden Trail Loop *(to skip this loop head left and follow the wide but overgrown single track as it dips down to a marshy area and then climbs to the return of the Tilden Trail)*.

Veer right to continue with the Tilden Trail, a two-track at this point. This mile-long loop is easier to follow than Sandi's or Minnie's but does include a pair of downhill runs and subsequent climbs in the first half. The trail then swings north and ends as a a gentle climb to a junction where Tilden Trail is posted as the *Main Trail*.

Continue straight toward "Cliff's Drive" and just beyond **Mile 4** you emerge at a paved road. Head left (north) to quickly arrive at a posted junction. By remaining on Cliff's Drive, you would quickly arrive at Cedar Lake, a beautiful body of water that is totally undeveloped.

The main trail departs Cliff's Drive to the left at the junction and quickly crosses a ravine on an unusual wood and iron bridge. Just beyond it you break out at a scenic view of a pond surrounded by marsh and then arrive at a posted junction with South Cedar Trail at **Mile 4.5**. Also posted here is a spur to a beaver dam at the north end of the pond.

The main trail to the Hill Street parking area continues straight (north), rolls through a series of hills and crosses under a pair of powerlines. None of the downhill runs are as steep as what you experienced on Tilden Trail. In the final half mile you pass a few more junctions, some posted as South Cedar Trail and Lizard Loop. Continue following the *Main Trail* which heads north and breaks out at the parking lot at **Mile 5**.

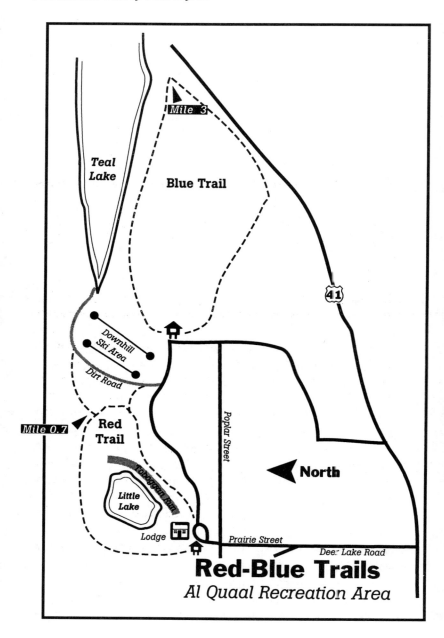

Teal Lake

Mile 3

Blue Trail

41

Downhill Ski Area

Dirt Road

Mile 0.7

Red Trail

Poplar Street

North

Toboggan Run

Little Lake

Lodge

Prairie Street

Deer Lake Road

Red-Blue Trails
Al Quaal Recreation Area

Al Quaal
Recreation Area

County: Marquette
Total Mileage: 4 miles
Terrain: Lakes and rocky cliffs
Fees: None
Difficulty: Easy

A half century ago the Finnish residents of Ishpeming went to the hills that is now the Al Quaal Recreation Area to do something most of us think is pretty crazy - ski jumping. On a ramp built on the side of a hill, these Finns would ski off the end of it and fly into the air before landing, or crashing, on Little Lake.

The ski jumpers have long since moved to the other side this historic mining town, to a place appropriately named Suicide Bowl, and now, instead of a ramp, the park features a toboggan run. There is also a small downhill ski area and 3 miles of cross country ski trails to keep little Yoopers entertained during those long U.P. winters.

In the summer, the trail system at Al Quaal Recreation Area is the perfect destination for a short after-dinner ride or an outing that involves the entire family. Both loops of the trail system are easy, with the Blue Trail being a half mile longer than the Red Trail. This route describes both trails as a single ride as they connect with unmarked trails.

Getting There: Ishpeming is 12 miles west of Marquette on US-41/M-28. From US-41 head north on Deer Lake Road and veer right onto Prairie Street. Parking and the park's impressive log shelter are on the northeast corner of Prairie and Poplar Street.

Information: Contact Marquette Country Visitors Bureau, 2552 US-41 West, Ste. 300, Marquette, MI 49855; ☎ (800) 544-4321. Or call the Ishpeming Parks Division at ☎ (906) 486-6181.

Red and Blue Trails

Distance: 4.3 miles
Trail: Wide single track

Begin at the park's log lodge, built in 1938 by the Ishpeming Ski Club. The Red Trail begins as an unassuming split in a row of pines to the left and quickly descends the same slope that the toboggan run utilizes. In less than a half mile the trail, a wide single track, passes an excellent view of Little Lake. Enjoy the view because soon you're grinding up a fairly significant climb. The climb is made in two stages, with the trail skirting some impressive rock cliffs after topping off.

At **Mile 0.7** the trail forks and you need to veer right. After a downhill run veer left at the next two forks, the second at **Mile 1** where you follow black and red arrows to another climb. This one tops off on some highbanks above the lake. The Red Trail finishes with short downhill run, where you veer right to the toboggan run and climb alongside it to the lodge and parking lot.

There are two ways to reach the Blue Trail. Before returning to the toboggan run on the Red Trail, an unmarked path veers off to the left and ends at the park's beach area on Teal Lake. From there you climb a dirt road past the ski slopes to the posted trailhead next to the tow rope shack on top.

You can also reach the Blue Trail by completing the Red Trail and simply following the park road east past the pavilion to the downhill ski area. The trailhead features a display map and is to the left of the parking area on top of the ski slope. If you're a downhill enthusiast, there are plenty of opportunities from this vantage point.

From the trailhead the Blue Trail begins with a fast downhill swoop through dark, dense pines. At **Mile 2.6** the downhill grade increases even more so you need to be in control here. *Please control your speed here as locals walk this trail in fair-weather months.* At **Mile 3** the trail veers to the right and turns into a two-track that parallels US-41. You then encounter the most sustained uphill of the ride, cresting it at **Mile 3.5**.

Swinging away from the highway a blue trail symbol steers you to the right at a fork into stand of hardwoods, pines and dense ferns. A downhill later and you're back at the trailhead. From here it's an easy pedal back to the car along the park road for a ride that totals 4.3 miles.

In a puddle and loving it! A mountain biker discovers just how deep some of the water holes are along the Wilson Creek Truck Trail.

Wilson Creek Truck Trail

County: Marquette
Total Mileage: 17.5 miles
Terrain: Waterfalls, stream crossings, Yellow Dog River
Fees: None
Difficulty: Moderate to strenuous

Perhaps one of the most intriguing areas for mountain biking in the central U.P. is the foothills of the Huron Mountains, just south of Big Bay. Bisected by County Roads 550 and 510, this scenic area is a rugged forest laced with trout streams, waterfalls and miles of old logging roads and obscure two-tracks.

It's best described as adventure mountain biking in which you use your bicycle to explore the backcountry. There are no directional arrows, mileage markers or cute names for technical sections in the woods north of Marquette.

There's not even a good map of the area. Cyclists use U.S. Geological Survey topographicals, known as quads, to navigate their way through the woods but do so knowing the maps were produced more than 20 years ago. It's inevitable you will encounter two-track roads not on the quads.

Before riding this area purchase the most detailed U.S.G.S. topos, the 7.5-minute quadrangle series of *Silver Lake Basin*, *Negaunee NW*, and *Buckroe*. Then pack a compass, a few pieces of survival gear in case you get totally lost and have to spend the night in the woods, and head down County Road 510 from Big Bay, stopping at the first two-track that looks inviting.

Most of the land in this area is either part of the Escanaba State Forest or owned by mining or logging companies that have opened it up to the public for tax purposes. Ride to your heart's content, discover rocky highpoints that give way to scenic views, tiptoe around puddles because you're not sure how deep they are, end the day by retracing your route back to CR 510.

The other way is to go with locals like Great Northern Adventures. The Marquette-based tour company offers both day trips for mountain bikers out of Big Bay and multi-day packages with accommodations at Thunder Bay Inn. Call the tour company at ☎ (906) 225-8687 for a brochure. Mountain bikes can also be rented in Big Bay at the North Country Outfitters store ☎ (906-345-9504).

The route described here is a 17.5-mile ride along both Wilson Creek Truck Trail and Bushy Creek Truck Trail, a pair of very rugged two-tracks. The loop is completed by following a portion of CR-510, a dirt road, and CR-550, a paved road with moderate traffic. You can pick up the loop from four different access points. By beginning on CR-510 past the west end of Bushy Creek Truck Trail, you can warm up with a long climb on the county road and then enjoy a wild downhill run at the beginning of Wilson Creek Truck

What follows is not a description of the route as has been done with other mountain bike trails in this book, but just the highlights and rough mileage to give you an idea of what to expect. You still need to purchase the proper topos and be prepared to do a little route finding along the way.

Getting There: From Marquette head north on CR-S50 toward Big Bay. Within 20 miles turn left onto CR-510 and head south for 6.5 miles. After crossing a bridge over the Yel-

Mountain bikers pause to enjoy Bushy Creek Falls, one of several that can be seen along the Wilson Creek Truck Trail ride.

low Dog River, look for a parking area on the left.

Information: Contact the Marquette Visitors Bureau, 2552 US-41 West, Suite 300, Marquette, MI 49855; ☎ (800) 544-4321. The Bureau's Marquette County Road and Recreation Map is especially useful for finding the trailhead to Bushy Creek Truck Trail on CR-510 but is not detailed enough once you are on the trail.

For a list of mountain bike trips with Great Northern Adventures contact the company at P.O. Box 361, Marquette, MI 49855; ☎ (906) 225-8687.

Wilson Creek Truck Trail

Distance: 17.5 miles
Trail: Two-tracks and county roads
Direction: Counter clockwise

From the steel bridge across scenic Yellow Dog River, head south on CR-510, a wide dirt road. Be careful on this road. Traffic is light but those who use it tend to clip along. At **Mile 1.7**, Big Pup Creek Falls, a series of small cascades, will appear on the left (east) side of CR-510. Beyond the falls the country road begins to climb, crosses a bridge over Big Pup Creek and continues to rise steadily.

At **Mile 2.5** the road tops off and passes a junction with Wilson Creek Truck Trail. The two-track is unmarked but is a major route that heads east (left), doubling as a snowmobile route during the winter. The first leg of this rutted two-track is a wild descent of more than a mile that crosses Little Pup Creek along the way. After that the trail levels out somewhat but the ride remains rough, with large puddles and washed-out sections to negotiate. Within three miles or so from CR-510 you pass a two-track that leads north toward Johnson Creek. Stay right and then veer left at the next pair of two-tracks.

Eventually you break out at Johnson's Road, a paved loop off of CR-550. Turn left on it to quickly come to CR-550 at **Mile 7.5**. It's a 4-mile ride along the paved shoulder of CR-550 before you can dip back into the woods on Bushy Creek Truck Trail. Be careful as the traffic can be moderately heavy at times and very fast.

Just after crossing a bridge over the Yellow Dog River, turn left on the first dirt road, reached at **Mile 11.5**. Bushy Creek Truck Trail begins as a dirt road that first passes Bear Lake and then skirts the Yellow Dog River. There are a surprising number of cabins and homes in the first half mile and mountain bikers need to respect their property and privacy.

Eventually, Bushy Creek Truck Trail turns from a road to a two-track and finally a trail so rugged that no four-wheel-drive

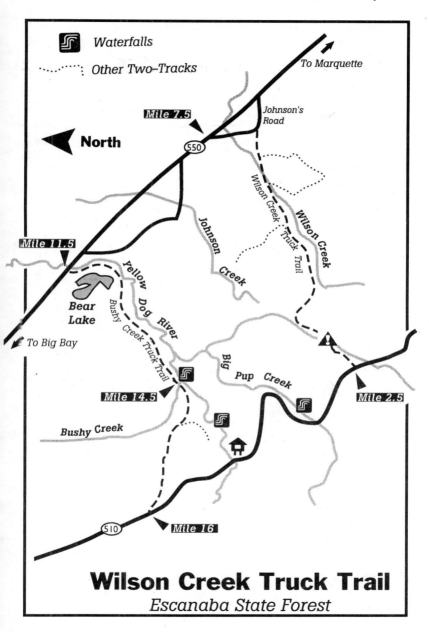

Waterfalls

Other Two–Tracks

North

Mile 7.5

To Marquette

Johnson's Road

550

Wilson Creek Truck Trail

Wilson Creek

Johnson Creek

Mile 11.5

To Big Bay

Yellow Dog River

Bushy Creek Truck Trail

Bear Lake

Big Pup Creek

Mile 14.5

Mile 2.5

Bushy Creek

510

Mile 16

Wilson Creek Truck Trail
Escanaba State Forest

vehicle, not even a Hummer, can follow it. You get a few more glimpses of the Yellow Dog, including one from a steep bluff above it before swinging away from the river almost 2 miles from CR-550.

After a notable climb, the trail descends and at roughly **Mile 14.5** passes the stone foundation of what appears to be an unfinished cabin in the middle of nowhere. Drop the bikes here and descend the slope to the left (south) and foot paths will lead you to Bushy Creek Falls. This is a stunning cascade that thunders 20 feet in a small, rocky gorge and ends in a series of rapids. Large boulders surround the river here and make it the perfect place to stretch out in the sun for an extended break.

Within a quarter mile of the falls is a major junction with another two-track. Veer right. Brushy Creek Truck Trail improves after this as it climbs to CR-510, reached at **Mile 16**.

Turn left (south) on CR-510 and the final leg is 1.5 miles of easy riding back to the steel bridge over the Yellow Dog River. If you have any energy left and want to view more waterfalls, leave the bikes and follow the hiking trail that heads east from the south side of the bridge. Within 0.75 miles of walking downstream you'll come to Yellow Dog Falls. This is another scenic cascade that is 50-feet wide and drops 30 feet around a massive boulder in the middle.

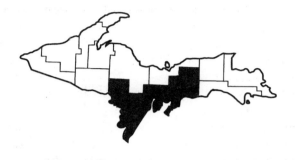

Central
Upper Peninsula

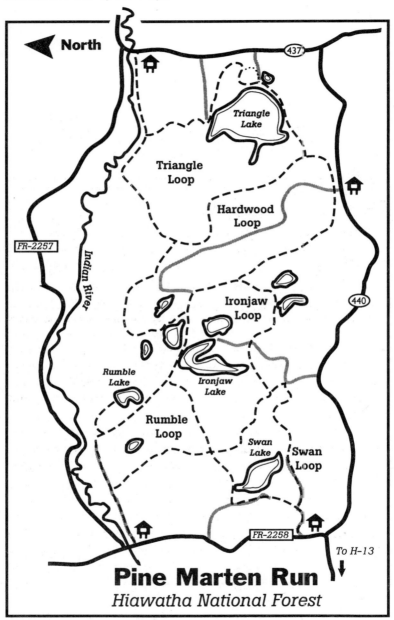

North

437

Triangle
Lake

Triangle
Loop

Hardwood
Loop

FR-2257

Indian River

Ironjaw
Loop

440

Ironjaw
Lake

Rumble
Lake

Rumble
Loop

Swan
Lake

Swan
Loop

FR-2258

To H-13

Pine Marten Run
Hiawatha National Forest

Pine Marten Run

County: Schoolcraft
Total Mileage: 26 miles
Terrain: Lakes, rolling forests, Indian River
Fees: None
Difficulty: Easy to moderate

Although four forest roads bisect it, the Ironjaw Semi-Primitive Area is virtually a non-motorized tract in the Hiawatha National Forest. Located 30 miles northwest of Manistique, the area is 5 miles wide and features Pine Marten Run, a 26-mile network of trails open to hikers, equestrians and mountain bikers.

The scenery is excellent. The trails pass through a wide variety of vegetative communities that include a dozen lakes, streams, the Indian River, gently rolling hills, bogs and wildlife openings. Wildlife encounters ranges from deer, beaver and waterfowl to possibly sighting an eagle or a black bear.

Pine Marten Run is composed of five loops with inter-connecting spurs and is accessed from four main trailheads off of County Roads 440 and 437, and Forest Road 2258. The area features three Adirondack-type shelters which allow mountain bikers to turn their ride into an unique overnight adventure in the fall when the bugs are gone.

There are also a handful of primitive drive-in campsites on

Swan Lake, Triangle Lake, Ironjaw Lake and Nineteen Lake that can be reserved in advance through the Manistique Ranger District. Called "dispersed campsites," these are isolated sites where you can pitch a tent overlooking a lake and directly access portions of Pine Marten Run.

In general the riding is relatively easy and the system, a mix of wide paths and two-tracks, is well posted. There is the occasional segment of single track and lots of mud holes and sand traps that will be encountered on any route. Also, keep in mind that the use of horses in the area leaves some trails pot-holed with hoof prints

The route described here is a combination of the Rumble Loop and the Ironjaw Loop, a ride of 9.4 miles that includes the most lakes, the best scenery and two of the three shelters. The halfway point in the ride is the shelter on Rim Lake, a great place to take an extended lunch break or even spend the night if you pack along a sleeping bag.

Getting There: From M-28 near Munising, head south on H-13 for 17 miles, past the trailhead to Bruno's Run and the posted entrance to Pete's Lake Campground. Head east on Country Road 440 for almost 4 miles and then north on Forest Road 2258 for 2 miles. Just before crossing the bridge over Indian River is one of the four trailheads and parking areas on the west side of the road.

Information: Contact Manistique Ranger District, Manistique, MI 49854; ☎ (906) 341-5666.

Rumble and Ironjaw Loops

Distance: 9.4 miles
Trail: Single track and two-track
Direction: Clockwise

From the trailhead parking area, cross FR-2258 and continue on a two-track that is open to motorized vehicles for the

One of the three Adirondack-type shelters that have been built along the Pine Marten Run in the Hiawatha National Forest

first mile. This two-track extends east through an open area that was cleared as part of a sharptail grouse management area. After passing a view of the Indian River, the two-track moves into a pine plantation and ends at a barrier gate.

Beyond the gate the trail becomes more of a wide path in the woods as it quickly swings south and at **Mile 1.3** arrives at the junction with a spur to Rumble Lake. The side trail to the lake is less than a half-mile long and ends at one of the three Adirondack-type shelters. The three-sided log shelter is on a low rise above the lake and makes for a serene place to spend an evening.

The main trail continues south past the junction where you endure a long climb, an almost equally long descent and then several smaller hills before arriving at a junction with the Ironjaw Loop at **Mile 2.4**. Veer left onto a true single track. This segment quickly climbs to a ridge between Ironjaw and Verdant lakes and briefly follows the crest to provide you views through the trees of both bodies of water. A wild downhill run takes you to the next junction near **Mile 3**. To the right, the trail leads to a pair of campsites lying between Ironjaw and Nineteen lakes and then to FR-2728, a two-track that is open to motorized vehicles.

This route continues left at the junction onto the single track that skirts Verdant Lake's east end. This section can be very muddy at times before you begin to climb away from the shoreline to the next junction at **Mile 3.6**. Veer right here.

Heading south now you continue along a wide path that within a half mile passes a pair of barrier gates to an old two-track road. A spur to Nineteen Lake is quickly passed and at **Mile 4.5** is a junction where the Ironjaw Loop splits from the Hardwood Loop. Veer right (west) to continue toward Rim Lake. The riding remains easy as you pass within view of Hub Lake and then Rim Lake. At **Mile 5.2** you reach a short spur to the Adirondack-type shelter on the northwest corner of Rim Lake.

Within a third of a mile from Rim Lake the trail crosses FR-2728 that is used by people in vehicles to reach the campsites on Ironjaw and Nineteen lakes. On the west side of the gravel road, the trail continues as a rough single track through the forest. This section is a little technical at times but within a third of a mile you are rewarded with a nice view of Ironjaw Lake's south end.

At **Mile 6.2** you reach the junction with Swan Loop. Veer right to continue north along a trail that is wider but soft at times and marred by hoof prints. The next junction is reached at **Mile 7** and is a four-way intersection. Continue straight.

This leg begins as a very distinguishable trail for the first mile but then is more difficult to follow after it enters a red

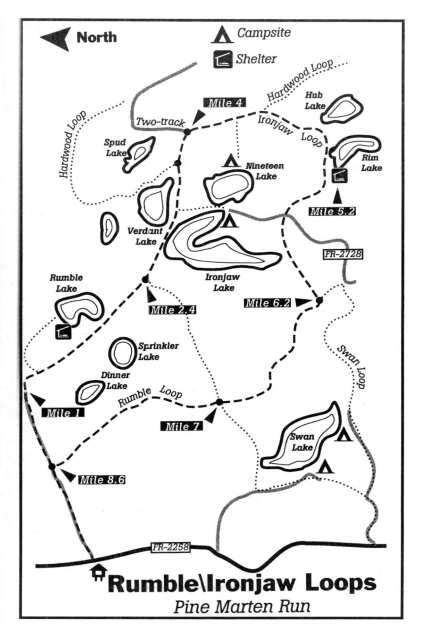

North

△ Campsite

▨ Shelter

Hardwood Loop

Mile 4

Two-track

Ironjaw Loop

Hub Lake

Hardwood Loop

Spud Lake

Nineteen Lake

Rim Lake

Mile 5.2

Verdant Lake

Ironjaw Lake

FR-2728

Rumble Lake

Mile 2.4

Mile 6.2

Sprinkler Lake

Swan Loop

Dinner Lake

Rumble Loop

Mile 1

Mile 7

Swan Lake

Mile 8.6

FR-2258

Rumble\Ironjaw Loops
Pine Marten Run

pine plantation, due to being re-routed in recent years. You now break out at the two-track road at **Mile 8.6** closer to its east end than to FR-2258. Head left (west) on the road and in less than a mile you will reach the trailhead and parking area.

Swan Loop

Distance: 3.8 miles

You can access this loop from FR-2258 just north of the intersection with CR-440. This segment begins with a 0.7-mile stretch of a two-track road to the popular dispersed campsites on Swan Lake. A barrier gate then prevents vehicles from traveling any further east on the loop. The terrain in this area is fairly level and composed of pine plantations interspersed with hardwood and hemlocks.

Hardwood Loop

Distance: 6.4 miles

This loop can be best accessed north of CR-440, where the trail intersects with FR-2728. Traversing the central portion of the Ironjaw Semi-Primitive Area, Hardwood Loop circles Spud Lake at the north end through a variety of vegetative types and topography.

Triangle Loop

Distance: 7.2 miles

There is a major trailhead and parking area on CR-4376, just after you cross the Indian River bridge. This is the longest segment in the system and at times also the wettest as it skirts several cedar swamps. There are also some hardwood ridges to climb while a mile of the loop's northern end parallels the Indian River and active beaver communities. The third Adirondack-type shelter is located on the Triangle Loop, overlooking the Indian River. The trail also passes near the dispersed campsites at the north and south ends of the lake.

Indian Lake Pathway

County: Schoolcraft
Total Mileage: 6 miles
Terrain: Flat to rolling forest
Fees: Donation
Difficulty: Easy

Located minutes from Palms Brook State Park, home of Michigan's largest spring, Indian Lake Pathway is a cross-country ski trail that is slowly being discovered by mountain bikers. Like so many other Upper Peninsula trails, this 6-mile system is lightly used through most of the summer, making it a good destination for a quiet ride in the woods where solitude is more important than scenery.

The pathway is ideally located for families visiting the Manistique area, especially those camping at the West Unit of the Indian Lake State Park. It's an easy ride from either the campground or popular Palms Brook State Park to the trailhead.

The system is composed of three loops of 1 mile, 3 miles and the longest at 4.5 miles. None of them are overly difficult but the backside of the third loop does feature a good climb up a ridge and then a series of rolling hills. The only drawback is that the area is crisscrossed by two-tracks and a dirt road. Although the system is well marked by junctions posts and blue pathway triangles, at times you will have to stop, look around and maybe even backtrack to find the last trail marker. For this reason the loops are best followed in a counter clockwise direction so trail markers will be facing you.

Getting There: From Thompson on US-2, head north on M-149 for 9 miles. The trailhead is west of the intersection of M-149 and County Road 455.

Information: Contact DNR Field Office, M-28, Shingleton, MI 49884; ☎ (906) 341-2518.

Indian Lake Pathway
Distance: 4.5 miles
Trail: Two-track, single track
Direction: Counter clockwise

The trail begins as a wide single track in a forest of mature hardwood and scattered pines. Be prepared for plenty of small deadfall that can rip out a computer wire, or worse, a spoke. From the trailhead display board you immediately cross the first of many two-tracks. Blue pathway triangles will keep you on course. The first leg is a level ride that winds through a beech-maple forest and reaches Post 2 at **Mile 0.4**.

Veer right to continue with Loop 2. In the next third of a mile the trail crosses three more two-tracks and can be tough to follow at times, especially in the fall when the leaves are down. Keep an eye out for the those blue diamonds and if you haven't seen one for a while backtrack. After the third two-track, the trail becomes more rolling and at **Mile 1.3** enters a confusing area where there has been some logging activity. Keep riding straight (west) and at **Mile 1.5** the trail will arrive at Post 3, on the edge of a dirt road.

Blue diamonds lead you right on the dirt road for 50 yards and then due south through a pine plantation to Post 4, reached at **Mile 1.7**. To continue onto the final loop you head right on a wide two-track briefly and then left onto a single track where

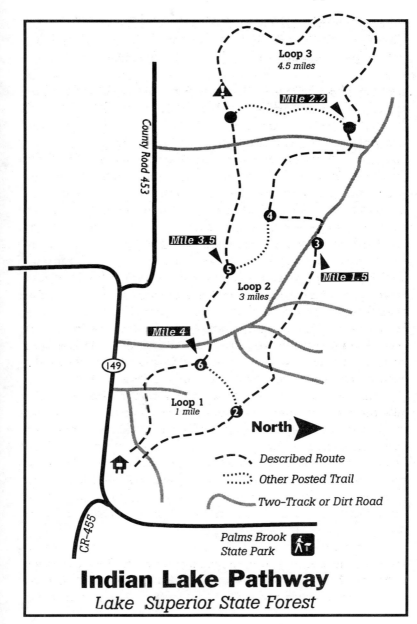

Loop 3
4.5 miles

Mile 2.2

County Road 453

4

Mile 3.5

5

3

Mile 1.5

Loop 2
3 miles

Mile 4

6

Loop 1
1 mile

2

North

- - - - *Described Route*

········· *Other Posted Trail*

——— *Two-Track or Dirt Road*

149

CR-455

*Palms Brook
State Park*

Indian Lake Pathway
Lake Superior State Forest

a *Loop 3* sign has been posted.

The trail becomes even more rolling now and at **Mile 2.2** you arrive at a two-track posted with a trail map and a bypass for skiers who want to skip the hills at the back of Loop 3. Veer right and at **Mile 2.6** you make the steepest climb that day and then ride through a delightful series of hills.

This is a fun and beautiful stretch of the pathway system. There are no obnoxious two-tracks to confuse you and at times you skirt a low ridge where you can see down into the forest on both sides. It ends with a steep downhill run to the posted south end of the bypass. Continue straight (east) for Post 5.

The trail widens here, crosses a couple of two-tracks but is well marked. Post 5 is reached at **Mile 3.5**. The riding remains easy but most of the two-tracks that can lead you astray are in the east half of the system. Keep your eyes open for blue diamonds. After re-crossing the dirt road, you reach Post 6 at **Mile 4**. Veer right.

In the final half mile the trail swings south and then east to emerge at the trailhead parking area. Again two-tracks can take you in the wrong direction if you miss the trail signs. One of them ends at paved M-149, in which case you need only to turn left to quickly return to your car.

Little Bay de Noc Recreation Area

County: Delta
Total Mileage: 2.5 miles
Terrain: Little Bay de Noc,
hemlock forest
Fees: Vehicle entry fee
Difficulty: Easy

In the late 1800's, residents in Gladstone could look across Little Bay de Noc and see giant hemlocks that towered above the shoreline. Locals called it Maywood and would row across the bay to enjoy picnics or camp overnight among the old growth pines. The spot became even more popular after a hotel was built at the turn of the century and ferries began transporting visitors from as far away as Chicago.

Thanks in part to that early tourism, the pines were spared the lumberman's wrath and today are the centerpiece of Little Bay De Noc Recreation Area. Built in 1990, the recreation area is part of the Hiawatha National Forest and includes a 36-site rustic campground, picnic area, swimming beach and boat launch.

There is also a 3.3-mile trail system with most of it open to mountain bikes. With its sandy beach, old growth pines and the shoreline campsites, Little Bay de Noc Recreation Area makes for an excellent camping destination where a family, with even its youngest mountain biker, can enjoy more than 2 miles of single track.

Getting There: Little Bay de Noc Recreation Area is located on the west shore of Stonington Peninsula. From Rapid River head 2 miles on US-2 east and then south 6 miles on County Road 513.

Information: Contact Rapid River District, 8181 US-2, Rapid River, MI 49878; ☎ (906) 4746442.

White Pine Trail

Distance: 3 miles
Trail: Single track
Direction: Clockwise

This route combines the Bayshore Trail and White Pine Trail for a 3-mile ride. The third trail at the recreation area is the Maywood History Trail, an interpretive pathway that mountain bikers should avoid riding on.

From the Hunter's Point Boat Launch you can pick up the north end of Bayshore Trail, which begins as a narrow single track in the woods and then quickly breaks out in the open day-use area. At the south end you re-enter the woods and at **Mile 0.6** arrive at the posted junction of the White Pine Trail. Veer left to ride through this old growth stand of hemlocks.

Just before **Mile 1** you cross the campground road and continue on the other side. This is a fun but easy segment that weaves through the trees. At **Mile 2** the trail re-crosses the campground road and ends in the series of sites known as Oaks Loop. Pick up the Bayshore Trail and head north, enjoying the views and breeze off Little Bay de Noc. The boat launch is reached at **Mile 3**.

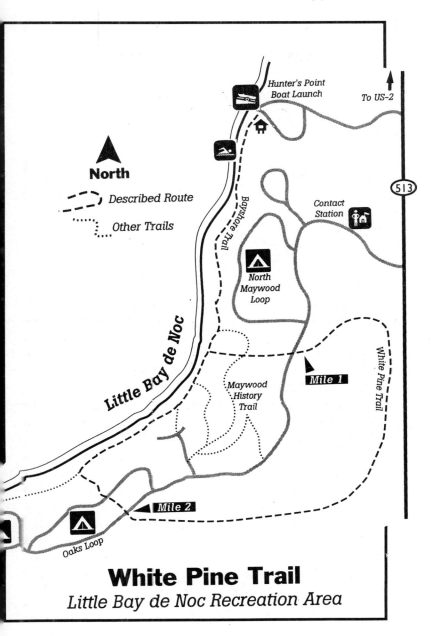

North

- – – Described Route
- ⋯⋯ Other Trails

Hunter's Point
Boat Launch

To US–2

513

Bayshore Trail

Contact
Station

North
Maywood
Loop

Little Bay de Noc

Mile 1

White Pine Trail

Maywood
History
Trail

Mile 2

Oaks Loop

White Pine Trail
Little Bay de Noc Recreation Area

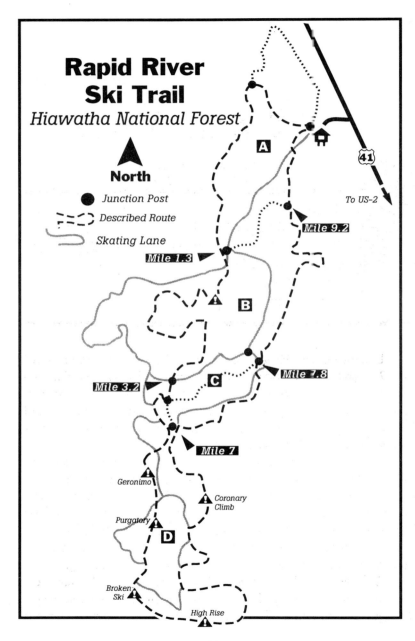

**Rapid River
Ski Trail**

Hiawatha National Forest

North

● Junction Post

Described Route

Skating Lane

A

Mile 9.2

To US-2

Mile 1.3

B

C

Mile 7.8

Mile 3.2

Mile 7

Geronimo

Coronary
Climb

Purgatory

D

Broken
Ski

High Rise

(41)

Rapid River Ski Trail

County: Delta
Total Mileage: 19 miles
Terrain: Rolling forested dunes and wetlands
Fees: None
Difficulty: Strenuous

Located in the Hiawatha National Forest, a short drive off US-2, Rapid River National Cross Country Trail is a good multi-loop system for those looking for a little solitude or an off-road challenge. Design, built and posted for Nordic skiing, Rapid River is a lightly used area by either mountain bikers or hikers during the rest of the year.

The 19-mile system is made up of four main loops (A, B, C, and D) along with two skating lanes that appear as wide trails during the summer. Loops A and B are fairly easy, but the back ones, especially Loop D, is a challenging, wild ride for hard-core riders and thrill seekers. This route is a 9.7-mile combination of Loops A, B and D with many opportunities to shorten it or bail out if the hills are too overwhelming.

Conveniently located near US-2 and US-41, the junction where you head north for the trail system, is the Rapid River Ranger District office. The national forest office is open from 8 a.m. to 5 p.m. Monday through Friday and can provide trail maps for this system and others in the area.

Getting There: From US-2, head north on US-41 for Marquette and within 6 miles of Rapid River is the posted trailhead on the west side of the road.

Information: Contact Rapid River Ranger District, 8181 US-2, Rapid River, MI 49878; ☎ (906) 474-6442.

Rapid River Ski Trail

Distance: 9.7 miles
Trail: Single track and two-track
Direction: Counter clockwise

From the trailhead three routes depart into the woods; a two-track road that serves as a shortcut to Loop B and two trails. Begin on the trail to the left that heads west for Post A.

In less than a half mile this wide trail reaches a post signifying the Tot Loop, a level route for young skiers. Veer left to continue on the A loop. The trail first winds through a mature pine forest and then into a swampy area. After the terrain develops a slight chop the trail reaches the well-posted intersection for Loop A and Loop B at **Mile 1.3**. Also nearby is the skating loop for skiers, but this ride remains on the main loops.

Continuing south on Loop B, you hit the first significant uphill at Mile 1.6 where sand may hamper your pedaling. The trail then becomes a narrow single track before climbing *Herringbone Hill*. You top off in a mixed forest of predominantly beech. If your tank is running low you can sit on the bench here and enjoy the overlook.

From the bench, you skirt a little ridge and near **Mile 2** hit the first downhill with a caution sign, called *Piece of Cake*, followed by another a quarter-mile later. At **Mile 2.7** you're treated to a scenic ridgetop ride where valleys slope away on both sides of you.

Like many mountain bike systems in the Upper Peninsula, Rapid River was built as a ski trail in which many of the hills have been named.

Keep to the left at a Y intersection with the skating lane at **Mile 3.2** to enjoy the downhill run of *Pike's Peak*. At the bottom you'll cruise past the skating trail and then climb to the intersection for loops B, C, and D on the top of the next ridge. Mountain bikers who have had their fill should return via loops C or B here, with Loop B being the easiest ride back.

This ride continues with Loop D because a sign on the trail cautions skiers that steep hills lie ahead and not to bank on an immediate rescue if you get injured. How can you pass up a loop like this? I couldn't. Veer right.

Loop D welcomes you with an immediate climb that tops off with a downhill *Caution!* sign at **Mile 3.5**. After quick down and up you hit a slope appropriately named *Geronimo* in which both Loop D and a skating loop descend side by side. The next significant downhill is called *Purgatory*, followed by *Outta Sight*, which bottoms out in a wet area if it has been raining. During such periods of bad weather, the best bet is to dismount and walk the trail for the next quarter mile. More wet areas quickly follow.

At **Mile 4** you begin to climb, which is good and bad. The climb gets you out of the swamps; but it's still climbing. After two more climbs, you're rewarded with a pair of downhills, the first a whoop-de-doo called *Broken Ski*. From the second you climb to a ridgeline where at **Mile 4.8** there is a scenic view of the area.

The next posted downhill is called *Bounce* which has you rocketing down into a lush pine stand. After a wet area at **Mile 5.6** you climb *High Rise*, a good test of strength and climbing acumen where in the middle you must negotiate a Y intersection. Veer right to stay on the main loop and top off on a ridge followed by more ridgeline pedaling.

After one more significant uphill, *Coronary Climb* (that for me turned into Coronary Walk), the trail pops out onto a dirt road at **Mile 6.6**. Follow the road for 100 yards then veer right with the trail into the woods to reach a junction between the skating lane and D Loop at **Mile 6.7**. If you are frizzled out at this point, follow the skating lane back, which is easier riding than the main loops.

Loop D veers right and reaches a posted intersection with Loop B at **Mile 7**. You've survived Loop D and can now breathe easier as the riding becomes considerably flatter for the remaining 2.7 miles back to the trailhead. At **Mile 7.8** you return to the posted intersection where Loop C merges into Loop B. Veer right.

At **Mile 9.2** you reach the posted junction where Loop B merges into the remainder of Loop A. Near the post are benches for the weary. But why rest? All that remains is the last leg of Loop A, an easy half-mile ride to the parking lot.

Days River Pathway

County: Delta
Total Mileage: 12 miles
Terrain: Rolling pine forests, fern meadows and Days River
Fees: Donations
Difficulty: Easy

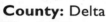

The Days River Pathway has its ups and downs; you'll be riding either up or down from the trailhead all the way to the Days River and back. But don't despair. The terrain is not overly steep and the way this trail was laid out it's easy to use the momentum from each downhill to propel your bike halfway up the next climb. The hills, in fact, are what is fun about this ride, providing plenty of grin-provoking downhill coasting.

The pathway, part of the Escanaba River State Forest, is a series of six loops that total 12 miles. The system has been re-routed and expanded over the years, including the addition of a 2.8-mile skating loop. DNR officials call the original outside loop an 8.8-mile ride but it measured out to be closer to 8.5 miles while a few older signs on the trail date back to when it was 9.2 miles.

This route, the 8.5-mile outside loop of the system, is a

ride that does include some pockets of thick sand. You can try to motor through these soft spots but it appears that most people simply dismount and wade through them.

The sand is a small inconvenience on an otherwise excellent, invigorating trail. Days River Pathway, a popular choice among local riders, is well maintained and clearly marked. This will allow you to concentrate less on your whereabouts and more on the pure fun of mountain biking...name y those hills.

Getting There: From Gladstone, head north on US-2/41 for 3 miles and then turn west on Days River Road. The trailhead is reached in 2.5 miles and is on the north side of the road.

Information: Contact Escanaba River State Forest, 6833 US-2/41, Gladstone, MI 49835; ☎ (906) 786-2354.

Days River Pathway
Distance: 8.5 miles
Trail: Single track
Direction: Counter clockwise

There is ample parking and a display map at the trailhead. You cross a wooden bridge to enter the trail system and then climb a high bank to reach a junction. The skating loop continues due north. This ride heads right to pass through a Civilian Conservation Corps pine plantation, which provides a quiet, pine-needle introduction to this part of the Escanaba River State Forest. Following the outside loop in a counter clockwise direction, you get a glimpse of the Days River Golf Course within a half mile and reach Post 2 at *Mile 1*. Stay right.

Within a third of a mile you descend to a place where a wide power line crosses the trail and for the first time view the Days River and even a small cascade. Blue diamonds will keep you on the trail as it swings northwest to skirt a small feeder creek, and at *Mile 1.7* reaches Post 3 at a second bridge. On the other side of the creek is a thick, momentum-sucking

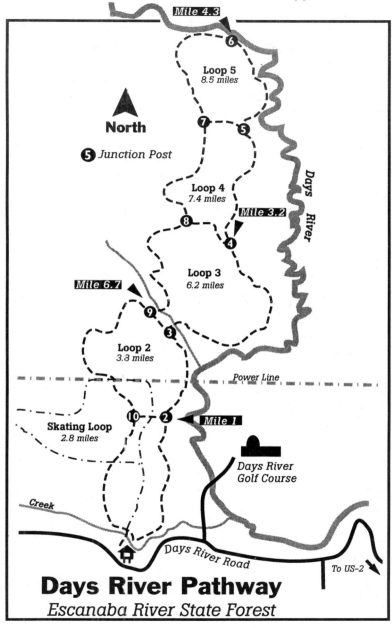

Central Upper Peninsula

Mile 4.3

Loop 5
8.5 miles

6

North

5 Junction Post

7

5

Loop 4
7.4 miles

Mile 3.2

Days River

8

4

Loop 3
6.2 miles

Mile 6.7

9

3

Loop 2
3.8 miles

Power Line

10

2

Mile 1

Skating Loop
2.8 miles

Days River
Golf Course

Creek

Days River Road

To US-2

Days River Pathway
Escanaba River State Forest

sand trap followed by a few small hills and another view of the Days River from a high bank at **Mile 2.2**. A pair of benches offers a respite for burning thighs.

You hit a major downhill in less than a half mile that bottoms out in a marshy area. At **Mile 3.2** you reach Post 4 and here can head left to return along the 6.2-mile loop or right to continue north along the outside loop. After two steep descents and a stiff climb between them, the trail weaves through a thick, chest-high fern meadow at **Mile 4** that smacks of jungle foliage. Be attentive here because it is difficult to see the trail under you. Consider keeping your weight on the back of the saddle to avoid any endos should your front tire suddenly stop.

Within a quarter mile is a spur to the right that leads to the banks of the Days River at a spot where a massive log jam clogs up the middle. Are those brook trout rising? From that spur the trail climbs to an overlook of the river then levels out as it skirts a ridge to begin the journey back the trailhead. Other views of the expansive valley soon open up.

The next stretch can be a challenge to follow at times because you cut through semi-open areas of either wetlands or areas that were logged in the past few years. Post 7 is reached at **Mile 5.5**, where the trail merges with a two-track, and Post 8 at **Mile 6**.

The segment between Post 8 and Post 9 is rated *Most Difficult* for skiers and features several hills posted with *Caution* signs, including a steep, sandy downhill that ends with a spin over a bridge to Post 9 at **Mile 6.7**. A steep, sandy uphill follows before you recross the power line corridor, which now doubles as part of the skating loop during the winter.

On the other side the trail moves into more sandy terrain as it crosses some two-tracks. Post 10 is reached at **Mile 7.7**, stay to the right and in less than a half mile you'll be skirting a bank overlooking the first creek of the day. The ride ends by crossing the wooden bridge back to the trailhead and parking area.

Cedar River Pathway

County: Menominee
Total Mileage: 8.5 miles
Terrain: Flat to rolling forest, Cedar River
Fees: Donation
Difficulty: Easy

The water from the well at the Big Cedar River State Campground is not to be missed. It's so cold, pure and sweet that locals come to the remote campground from miles around to fill up large bottles and take it home with them.

It tastes best, however, just after you finish a ride along the Cedar River Pathway. This state forest pathway is a very clean, easy-to-follow trail system, making it ideal for beginners. It's also a good trail for those of us who like to use our mountain bikes as a way to enjoy the sights and smells of the forest.

The 8.5-mile system is a 7-mile peripheral trail with three crossover spurs that allow you to ride four different loops. Loops I through 3 are predominantly in mature stands of hardwoods and pines and twice break out at the Cedar River. The fourth loop crosses over River Road and winds through an area that was actively logged in 1994. The ride described below is the peripheral route.

Both the well and the pathway trailhead are located in Big Cedar River Campground, a pleasant facility of 17 rustic sites. Four of the sites are right on the banks of the river where you can pitch your tent in the shade of towering pines and spend your post-ride cool-down watching trout rise. This is an excellent place to set up camp and spend a day or two mountain biking, trout fishing and relaxing.

Getting There: From M-35, just north of the town of Cedar River, turn west onto River Road, where there is state forest campground sign. Follow River Road in a northwest direction for 6 miles to the posted campground entrance.

Information: Contact Escanaba River State Forest, 6833 US-2/41 and M-35, Gladstone, MI 49837; ☎ (906) 786-2351.

Cedar River Pathway

Distance: 7 miles
Trail: Single track
Direction: Clockwise

The main trailhead is in a parking lot, reached before you enter the campground itself. Head left on the campground road, which skirts the Cedar River and then leads you into the campground. Among the sites is Post 1, reached at **Mile 1**, where you enter the forest on a wide single track. After passing an interpretive sign pointing out a giant white pine, a short climb brings you to Post 2, reached at **Mile 1.4**.

Head left to continue with the perimeter of the system. The trail twists and turns, develops a chop and leads you to a downhill that bottoms out in a cedar swamp filled with ferns most of the summer. It's a definitive change in scenery compared to the sparse hardwood forest up to this point. The first glimpse of the Cedar River is reached at **Mile 1.8,** at a spot where you can sit on a high bank and watch the current sweep through. **Post 3** is a quarter mile away.

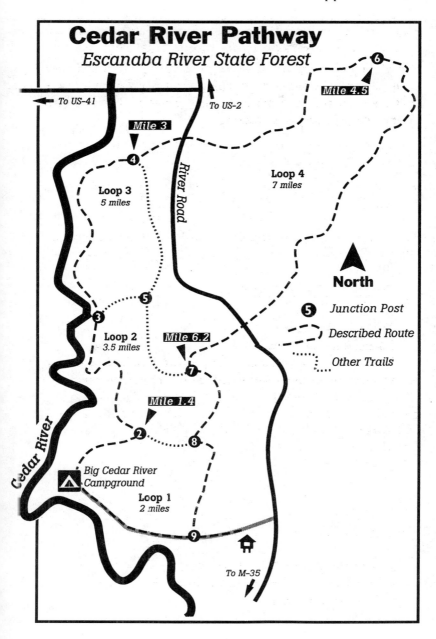

Cedar River Pathway
Escanaba River State Forest

To US–41

To US–2

Mile 3

Mile 4.5

River Road

Loop 3
5 miles

Loop 4
7 miles

North

Loop 2
3.5 miles

Mile 6.2

5 Junction Post

Described Route

Other Trails

Mile 1.4

Big Cedar River
Campground

Loop 1
2 miles

Cedar River

To M–35

Veer left for Post 4. The ride levels out and the trail narrows as it meanders and twists through the trees. I noticed numerous ground-dwelling spider webs here, and if you catch the trail in the morning the dew will dance magically off them as you ghost by. At **Mile 2.8** is a short downhill bottoming out at a bridge across a wet area. The bridge is best walked. From the other side you break out at another view of the river with a bench along the bank.

Post 4 is reached at **Mile 3**. Veer left toward Post 6 to continue on Loop 4. Closed in the 1994 due to logging, this loop is open and ready for adventurous mountain bikers. And you'll have to be a little adventurous as the trail narrows and becomes a close-quarters ride through overgrown brush. There is also a couple of lengthy water crossings to deal with.

You quickly arrive at River Road, where blue DNR pathway triangles lead you right back into the woods on the other side. Loop 4 begins with a bit of climbing and then skirts a ridgeline before emerging into a more open area. There was definitely a logging operation here, but many trees still remain, thanks to the method of selective harvesting that was used.

You'll climb up a few more ridgelines and then enter a large fern meadow at **Mile 4**. The trail is very overgrown here and can be hard to pick up at times. After another patch of boggy bottomland, the trail enters a half mile of tight pedaling through a tunnel of trees, where you'll have to know when to duck. Post 6 is reached at **Mile 4.5**.

Another wet area follows and, unfortunately, the trail, now an old logging road, heads right through it. Once past this water hazard there are a couple more minor ones, but the bottom is surprisingly firm. Loop 4 finishes with a leisurely pedal through a sparse forest back to River Road. On the other side Post 7 is reached within a quarter mile at **Mile 6.2**. Head left to return to the trailhead.

Veer right onto the rolling forested terrain and soon you'll be faced with the most significant climb of the day. It's followed

Cedar River Pathway is one of three river trail systems clustered around Escanaba that offer a rolling terrain and numerous overlooks of the rivers themselves. The other two are Rapid River Ski Trail and Days River Pathway.

by a gentle downhill run to Post 8, reached at **Mile 6.6**, where there is a vault toilet and benches. Continue on the main trail to meander along a rolling, narrow single track and break out at the campground road and Post 9. A quarter mile to the left is the trailhead and parking lot.

The end of Lake Mary Plains Pathway features a long boardwalk that crosses a wetland area at the north end of Glidden Lake. Opportunities to view wildlife are excellent along this section of the trail.

Lake Mary Plains Pathway

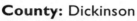

County: Dickinson
Total Mileage: 9.3 miles
Terrain: Rolling forests,
Glidden Lake
Fees: Donation
Difficulty: Moderate

   Since being partially destroyed by a forest fire in 1983, Lake
Mary Plains Pathway has been restored as one of the finest
cross country ski trails in Dickinson County. A portion of its
first loop has also been upgraded into a handicapped-accessible nature trail. Mountain bikers, however, have been slow
to discover this trail system.

   The pathway is comprised of three loops that total more
than 9 miles, with the perimeter being a 7.3-mile ride. Loop 3
has a tendency to be wet and sandy in spots and, having been
recently logged, is not nearly as interesting. But the first two
loops can be combined into a fun ride that is hilly in stretches
and very scenic at the end. The entire system is extremely well
marked with trail maps at almost every junction.

   The trailhead is located in Glidden Lake Campground, a
rustic state forest facility with 22 sites, including 10 overlooking the water. There is also a day-use area with a small sandy

beach where you can quickly cool down after the ride with a jump into this beautiful lake.

Getting There: From Crystal Falls, head east on M-69 for 4 miles and then south on Lake Mary Plains Road to Glidden Lake Campground. Park in the day-use area and ride into the campground to where the trailhead and display board.

Information: Contact Copper Country State Forest, 1420 US-2 West, Crystal Falls, MI 49920; ☎ (906) 875-6622.

Lake Mary Plains Pathway

Distance: 7.3 miles
Trail: Single track
Direction: Clockwise

From the trailhead in the campground, the pathway begins as an easy single track in a semi-open forest, reaching Post 1 in a third of a mile. Veer left to continue on Loop 2 and the perimeter route. You make your first small climb in another half mile and reach Post 2 where the trail crosses a two-track road that is a snowmobile route in the winter.

The next stretch of trail is posted *Most Difficult* for skiers and gets into some rolling terrain. There are two steep downhills on the way to Post 3, with the first one featuring a bypass route. Post 3 is reached at **Mile 1.2** where the trail crosses another two-track. On the other side is another pair of steep downhills and climbs.

The pathway crosses that two-track road once again and returns to it a third time at Post 4 near **Mile 2**. To continue on Loop 2 follow the two-track for a third of a mile to the right (west) to Post 6, where a single track re-enters the woods. Keep in mind there are an awful lot of logging roads in the southern half of the pathway, and its easy to get turned around while following them.

To ride Loop 3, you cross the two-track road at Post 4 and

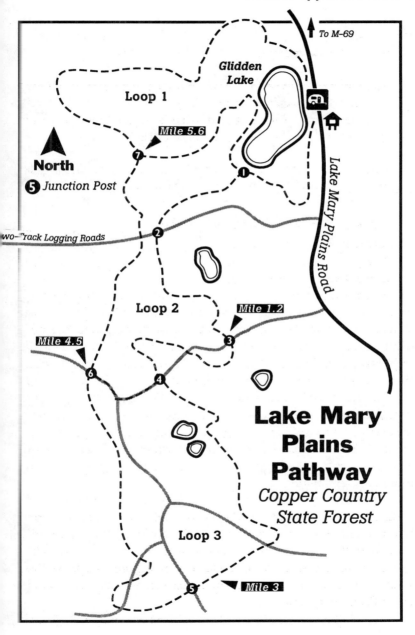

Central Upper Peninsula

To M-69

Glidden Lake

Loop 1

Mile 5.6

North

5 Junction Post

wo-Track Logging Roads

Lake Mary Plains Road

Mile 1.2

Loop 2

Mile 4.5

Lake Mary Plains Pathway

Copper Country State Forest

Loop 3

Mile 3

continue south on the trail through the stand of aspen sap-
lings. Loop 3 is rated *More Difficult* for skiers and is a rolling
ride that within a quarter mile swings past a boggy pair of ponds.
It then heads west and crosses three two-track roads, the second one featuring Post 5 reached just past *Mile 3*. The trail
swings north, crosses the third two-track road two more times
and then reaches Post 6 and Loop 2 at *Mile 4.5*.

The next leg is fun. You enter a mature forest and then
enjoy a fast downhill where its possible to build up enough
speed to almost reach the top of the ensuing climb. Eventually
you cross a two-track road and then move into a clearing that
appears to be a result of the 1983 forest fire. Posts with blue
blazes navigate you to the next junction. Post 7 is reached at
Mile 5.6 and has a bench and a skier's shelter, complete with a
picnic table.

The last segment of the trail is the northern half of Loop 1
back to the campground. You begin in a clearing of rolling terrain, then return to a mature forest on a trail that is wider and
more hard-packed than it has been all day. Along the way a
dozen interpretive signs have also been erected, most of them
discussing the various species of trees flying past you.

After a good downhill run that bottoms out in a sandtrap,
you reach a boardwalk in a tamarack swamp at *Mile 6.4*. It's a
scenic area but an even more interesting boardwalk is crossed
near the end. This one is almost 100 yards long through the
swamp at the north end of Glidden Lake. From the boardwalk
a handicapped-accessible gravel path leads into the day-use area
of the campground.

Fumee Lake Natural Area

County: Dickinson
Total Mileage: 9.5 miles
Terrain: Fumee lakes and an abandoned mine
Fees: None
Difficulty: Easy

Just northwest of Norway is what some people call the last unspoiled body of water in the Midwest because it's never been touched, not in this century at least.

In the early 1900s, when Norway was a booming mining center, the city council designated the 478-acre, spring-fed Fumee Lake and an adjacent 28-acre lake known as Little Fumee as the town's water source. They posted no trespassing signs and hired a caretaker to make sure it remained off-limits to fishermen, boaters, all users and to any development. It's been that way ever since.

But in 1988 Norway choose to drill a community well, a more cost-effective solution to their drinking water needs. Almost immediately a controversy erupted over what to do with this precious real estate. Developers were drooling over the thought of building high-priced homes along the shoreline. Others eyed cutting the mature timber or developing a gravel pit at one end. The residents of Dickinson County just wanted to preserve it and soon a Save-The-Lake movement began, resulting in the creation of Fumee Lake Natural Area, a 1,000-acre preserve.

This is a rare park. The two lakes combine for more than five miles of undeveloped shoreline. At 1,500 feet, the ridges are some of the highest in the county. There are 270 species of plants, including rare walking ferns and five types of orchids, 26 species of mammals that live there and dozens of springs in which cold, clear water bubbles out of the ground year-round.

The only development in this non-motorized area is a trail system around the lakes, which is open to mountain biking, and a gravel parking area. The trail system is composed of three loops; a 7-mile Big Fumee Lake Loop, a mile-long Little Fumee Lake Loop and a 2-mile South Ridge Loop that climbs to almost 1,300 feet.

This route is a combination of all three loops, resulting in an 8-mile ride along both single track and segments of two-track. Although there is some climbing and a little mud at the west end of the lake, this is a very easy and scenic outing.

Getting There: From US-2, between Norway and Quinnesec, head north on Upper Pine Creek Road (County Road 396) for 1.5 miles to the posted entrance of the park.

Information: Contact Dickinson County Tourism Association, 600 South Stephenson Ave., Iron Mountain, MI 49801; ☎ (800) 236-2447.

Big Fumee Lake Pathway
Distance: 8 miles
Trail: Two-track
Direction: Clockwise
From the parking lot, you ride around a locked gate and head up a gravel road to quickly reach a junction. Head left,

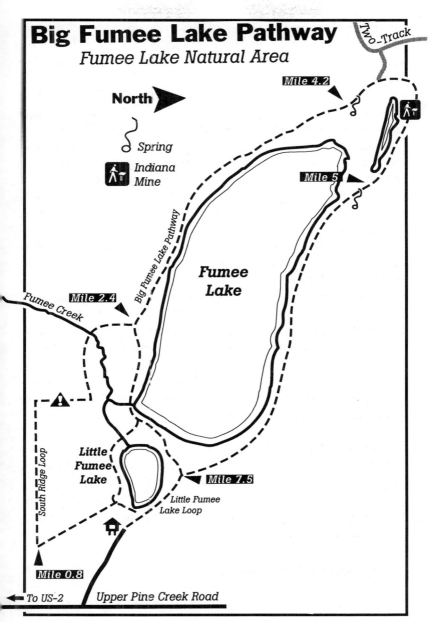

Big Fumee Lake Pathway
Fumee Lake Natural Area

North

Spring

Indiana Mine

Mile 4.2

Two-Track

Mile 5

Fumee Lake

Fumee Creek

Mile 2.4

Big Fumee Lake Pathway

South Ridge Loop

Little Fumee Lake

Mile 7.5

Little Fumee Lake Loop

Mile 0.8

To US-2   Upper Pine Creek Road

toward the canoe portage, and within a 100 yards the main trail swings sharply away from an imposing log fence with a bypass. This is the start of the 2-mile South Ridge Pathway.

The trail crosses a powerline right-of-way and begins a steady climb into the woods, reaching a posted junction at **Mile 0.8.** Here the trail swings sharply right, resumes the climb and finally tops off at 1,300 feet at **Mile 1.2.** The rest of the loop is a wild, almost mile-long downhill run. After bottoming out you cross a scenic little stream in a stand of cedar via a foot bridge and arrives at Big Fumee Lake Pathway at **Mile 2.4.**

Head left on the main trail, a wide two-track where Fumee Lake is visible through the trees. Within a mile you ride under a powerline, and at **Mile 3.7** the pathway leaves the two-track it was following and becomes a wide single track in the woods. You dip and weave briefly and then come to a stretch that is generally wet and very muddy throughout the summer. That's due to a spring that appears as a small pipe from the ground at **Mile 4.2**, with water constantly gurgling out.

This section of the trail lies outside of the city-owned natural area and is on CFR land, the reason for the lack of signage here. After tiptoeing your way around the spring, turn right at the first trail and then right again onto a wide single track with a hardpacked surface. Within a quarter mile of the spring you should be passing the abandoned Indian Mine, a huge shaft of rusty metal.

After passing a pond, the trail leaves CFR and re-enters the natural area, which is posted at **Mile 5.** The trail becomes a two-track again and soon Fumee Lake comes into view.

The best views of the water are along this stretch of the north shore. At one point you also pass a spur that leads down to the water. At **Mile 7.5** you reach a posted junction and merge onto Little Fumee Lake Pathway. Stay left and you'll quickly ride past the lake itself, another scenic body of water. The parking lot is just down the trail and reached at **Mile 8.**

Iron Mountain City Park

County: Dickinson
Total Mileage: 2.2 miles
Terrain: Forested hills
Fees: None
Difficulty: Easy

This is one ride where you're guaranteed to see wildlife because in the middle of Iron Mountain City Park is a deer yard. Within the fenced hillside slope are often up to a dozen deer, some of them bucks sporting impressive racks by September.

The rest of this park in the middle of Iron Mountain is also hilly, and winding through it is a 3.5-kilometer system of ski trails. The park is so hilly, in fact, that it served as the site of the city's first ski jump ramps before they were moved to Pine Mountain.

From spring through fall you can also use the trails for mountain biking. This is a place for a workout, not a scenic ride in the woods. The trails are wide, the mileage is limited and the scenery consists of stopping to look at those deer. But a few climbs are steep enough to get your heart pumping and leave your legs shaking if you ride the course a few times.

Getting There: From US-2 in downtown Iron Mountain, turn south on A Street and follow it to the entrance of the park. The park road exits at B Street, which can then be followed north to return to US-2.

Information: Contact the Tourist Association of Dickinson County, 600 S. Stephenson Ave., Iron Mountain, MI 49801; ☎ (800) 236-2447.

Iron Mountain City Park

Distance: 2 miles
Trail: Wide ski trails

When you enter the park, follow the road past the deer yard and up the hill to a parking area. This is the trailhead for skiers in the winter as well as kids who go sledding in the deep pit at the foot of the parking lot. A wide trail departs west and climbs a slope above the sledding area. Struggle through the sandy area at the top and then swing left to a mowed trail.

You are immediately greeted with a downhill run through a stand of pine that quickly bottoms out and then begins climbing. You emerge back at the sand trap at the top.

Head toward the parking lot but veer left at the next junction for another fun downhill run in the forest. You pass a crossover trail then bottom out near the park fence. The trail swings right (east) here and shortly you emerge near the park road and deer yard. See any big bucks? The trail then swings sharply west and begins to climb the hill. The parking lot is reached at **Mile 1** of the ride.

The second half of the ride is the park's Easy Loop. From the parking lot cross the soccer field and look for the wide mowed trail at its southeast corner. This loop begins with a nice dip and then gradually descends to B Street. You swing back west and gradually climb back to the soccer fields, which you can cross again to return to your car. If you need more of a workout, ride the loops again. If not, then go feed the deer.

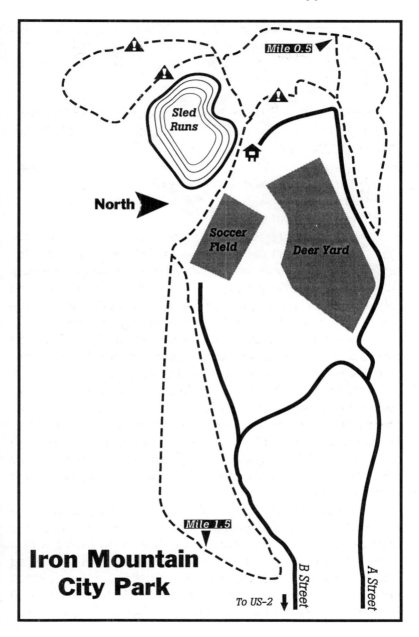

Mile 0.5

North

Sled
Runs

Soccer
Field

Deer Yard

Mile 1.5

**Iron Mountain
City Park**

To US-2

B Street

A Street

The scenery at Piers Gorge includes the wildest whitewater in Michigan and rafts full of thrill-seekers running the rapids in the summer.

Piers Gorge Trail

County: Dickinson
Total Mileage: 1.5 miles
Terrain: Menominee River and spectacular waterfalls
Fees: None
Difficulty: Easy to moderate

The Piers Gorge Scenic Area is a stretch of the Menominee River that includes Class V rapids, drops and waterfalls. It's a paradise for rafters and kayakers and they arrive from across the Midwest to experience this whitewater challenge.

Along the north side of the gorge is a point-to-point trail built and maintained by Wisconsin Power and Light and Norway/Vulcan Civic Club. Although roundtrip on the trail is only a 3-mile ride, the scenery is so spectacular you'll constantly be stopping to admire it. Arrive on a Saturday when you can watch rafters run the rapids on guided trips and this trail becomes a delightful two or three-hour event.

The route was built as a foot path and is a wide trail, but it can still be tricky for mountain bikers due to the many large rocks on a pair of climbs and descents in the first half mile. If riding with family or children, simply plan on walking these sections.

Getting There: From downtown Norway, 9 miles east of Iron Mountain, head south on US-8. Within a mile turn west on the paved road at the large Piers Gorge Scenic Area sign. The paved will turn to dirt and end at the trailhead.

Information: Contact the Tourist Association of Dickinson County, 600 S. Stephenson Ave., Iron Mountain, MI 49801; ☎ (800) 236-2447.

Piers Gorge Trail

Distance: 3 miles roundtrip
Trail: Wide path

Piers Gorge picked up its name from the wooden piers that lumber companies built in the river here to slow up the current and thus the timber they were floating to mills on Lake Michigan. There are four piers posted along the trail; each is a spur to a stretch of the river's spectacular whitewater.

From the parking lot a wood-chip trail heads west and quickly crosses a foot bridge and arrives at First Pier. The spur here leads you to mild stretch of rapids. The trail continues west, becomes more of a hard-packed dirt path and makes its first rock-strewn climb. You top off at the Second Pier, a spot where the whitewater is much more intense.

From the Second Pier the trail climbs again along a rock-strewn course that can be very challenging to novice mountain bikers. You top off at the Third Pier at **Mile 0.5**. This is the spot to view Misicot Falls, an incredible 10-foot drop in the river. If there are any rafters on the river that day this is where you want to watch them.

From the Third Pier, the trail makes a two-stage descent, where again you have to be careful of the rocks. It then levels out and within a third of a mile swings away from the whitewater to become a quiet ride in the forest. At **Mile 1** you cross a power line right-of-way and come to a V junction in the trail. Blue diamonds lead you down the right fork to the Fourth Pier, the beginning of the whitewater, reached at **Mile 1.5**. The official trail ends at the Fourth Pier.

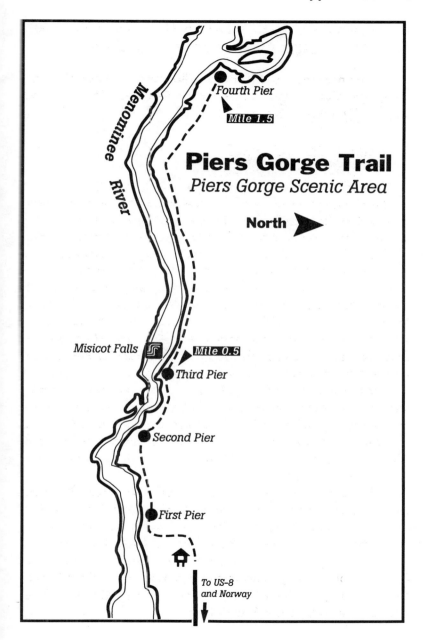

Fourth Pier

Mile 1.5

Piers Gorge Trail
Piers Gorge Scenic Area

North ▶

Menominee River

Misicot Falls

Mile 0.5

Third Pier

Second Pier

First Pier

To US-8
and Norway

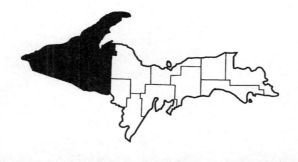

Western
Upper Peninsula

George Young Recreation Complex is an ideal desitnation for families and others new to the sport of mountain biking due to the easy and wide trails.

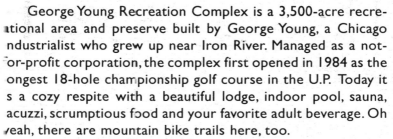

George Young Recreation Complex

County: Iron
Total Mileage: 12 miles
Terrain: Hardwood forest, rigdelines, scenic views
Fees: Daily trail fee
Difficulty: Easy

George Young Recreation Complex is a 3,500-acre recreational area and preserve built by George Young, a Chicago ndustrialist who grew up near Iron River. Managed as a not-⁻or-profit corporation, the complex first opened in 1984 as the ongest 18-hole championship golf course in the U.P. Today it s a cozy respite with a beautiful lodge, indoor pool, sauna, acuzzi, scrumptious food and your favorite adult beverage. Oh yeah, there are mountain bike trails here, too.

In 1994, the lodge was built and 15 miles of cross country ski trails were added with the system split on the north and south side of County Road 424. Eventually the southern trail system was closed to skiers, due to right-of-way problems with snowmobile trails and roads, but opened to mountain bikers in the summer.

This is not a destination for hardcore mountain bikers. There are many more challenging and wilderness-like trails systems to explore in the western half of the U.P.

This facility is perfect, however, for when you're touring the U.P with a non-biking companion, whether it is your best buddy, wife or kids. You can rent bikes on-site, most of the trails are easy, and afterwards soak away those sore muscles in the complex's jacuzzi or sauna. And once you are away from the golf course the complex is a pleasant wooded tract that includes mixed hardwoods, scenic views, ridgelines and mostly hardpacked trails with some rocks.

Getting There: George Young Recreational Complex is located on Chicagon Lake, eight miles east of Iron River. From Iron River take County Road 424 east or M-189 south and follow the signs. Pay for the trail pass in the golf shop, and they will provide a trail map and directions to the trailhead.

Information: For more information call the George Young Recreational Complex at ☎ (906) 265-3401. For a list of accommodations in the area, call the Iron County Tourism Council at ☎ (800) 255-3620.

Southern Trail System
Distance: 9.3 miles
Trail: Two-track and single track.
Direction: Counter clockwise

From the lodge, head over to the trailhead near the cart barn and then begin by following the cart path between the 18th and 10th greens to an old railroad grade. Head south on the grade, crossing the entrance road and CR-424 and arriving at a trail sign at **Mile 1**. To the right is a trail to Post B, while just down the grade to the left is the start of the Minnie Lake Loop, a flat trail that provides an ideal warm up.

This pathway enters a hardwood forest dominated by beech and aspen trees and quickly arrives at a "Y" intersection. Head left to view Minnie Lake at **Mile 1.5** and then continue along

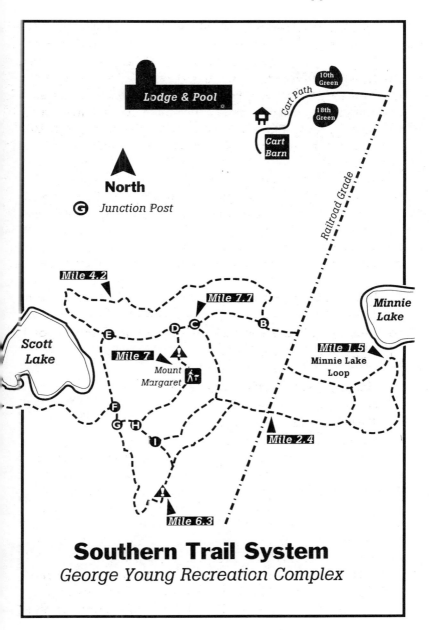

North

G *Junction Post*

Lodge & Pool

Cart Path

10th Green

18th Green

Cart Barn

Railroad Grade

Mile 4.2

Mile 7.7

Minnie Lake

Mile 1.5
Minnie Lake Loop

Scott Lake

Mile 7

Mount Margaret

E

D C

B

F

G H

I

Mile 2.4

Mile 6.3

Southern Trail System
George Young Recreation Complex

the back of the loop where there is a slight roll. Although there is no signage at the second intersection, take a left to continue the loop. Minnie Lake Loop ends back at the railroad grade at **Mile 2.4**.

You could continue straight onto the main trail system but it is better to return to Post B. By riding counter clockwise you reduce the number of climbs endured. Backtrack up the grade and at **Mile 2.7** a trail sign will point you to Post B.

This is the heart of southern trail system that is open to mountain bikes. Almost immediately you enter a segment of the Wolf Track Nature Trail and pass interpretive signs explaining a bog's origin and the benefits of bats. At Post B, veer right onto the more difficult loop. Wolf Track Nature Trail also follows this section of the trail so you will pass white-and-black mountain bike trail signs, more interpretive plaques, even a chickadee feeding area where the birds may land on your hand to eat. Try it, there's feed provided.

The trail becomes more heavily wooded and passes another educational area that challenges you to identify hemlock, birch, and assorted other hardwoods surrounding you. Just before **Mile 4** is the first real elevation change - upwards- but the ground is firm here and the pedaling relatively easy.

A quarter mile later the interpretive loop heads left while this ride continues straight to follow the peripheral loop and skirt Scott Lake. You'll face a gradual climb for a third of a mile while dodging rock eruptions as the trail becomes rockier along a ridgeline. But try to glance into surrounding vegetation occasionally. There's a lot of deer in this area, and you may be able to hear or possibly see them bounding off in the distance. This was the site of an old logging operation and the numerous tree stumps in the area create an eerie feeling at times.

While descending the ridge at **Mile 4.8**, you'll cut across a two-track, probably an old rail grade, and then take a left. A few hundred yards later you'll come to Post E, and veer right to continue south along Scott Lake. Post F contains a spur to the right which will provide more views of Scott Lake, but quickly dead-ends. At Post G you can steer left at the intersection to bail out of the ride and begin the trek back.

This route continues straight (south) to enter the most difficult segment of the trail. You'll climb a gradual hill for the next half mile, topping off at one of the highest elevations in the area. The trees and their foliage, however, hinder the view. But the view opens up halfway down the following descent and those carrying a camera may want to pause for a few frames' worth of scenic memories. There are plenty of deer in this area that occasionally can be seen loping away from you. This downhill is a long one and bottoms out at *Mile 6.3* in a thickly-forested bottomlands.

Directional arrows mark the trails at the next intersection. To the right you can head back to the Minnie Lake area, or left to continue with this ride and quickly reach Post I. Turn right on to Intersection I for the quickest return to the railroad grade.

This ride, however, heads left to check out Mt. Margaret, reached via Post H, a quarter mile away. It's a two-stage climb to the top with a plateau sandwiched in the middle. At *Mile 7* you'll reach the summit, where a Caution sign warns you of the ensuing downhill. Just as you start the descent there is a spur on your right that leads a short way to a plaque about Mt. Margaret, which was named by George Young after his first wife. The sign discusses contemplation and quiet places in which the universe can be contemplated in awe. Head back to the main trail, and a scrumptious downhill later you are back on the interpretive trail at Post D, an intersection on a two-track.

At *Mile 7.7* the trail divides at Intersection C and you can make a right for some more riding into the southern part of the system, or head left toward the parking lot. The trail at this point is an old logging road until you reach the railroad grade at *Mile 8.3*. At the grade, head north to bactrack the first mile back to the cart barn trailhead for a ride of 9.3 miles.

To Iron River

Forest Road 101

Brennan Lake

Brennan Lake Loop

Mile 2

Ge-Che Trail
Lake Ottawa Recreation Area

Water Treatment Plant

Ge-Che Loop

Lake Ottawa

Mile 4.5

Hagerman Lake

Covenant Point Bible School

Swamp

Hagerman Lake Road

Mile 9

Mile 5.2

Mile 7.3

North

Loggers Loop

● Junction Post

⌐⌐⌐ Described Route

Ge-Che Trail

County: Iron
Total Mileage: 11 miles
Terrain: Lakes, rolling forests
Fees: None
Difficulty: Moderate to strenuous

The Ge-Che Trail is actually only one of four loops within the Lake Ottawa Recreation Area, a scenic place to spend a weekend. But it's such a fun name that mountain bikers and skiers often refer to the entire system as the Ge-Che Trail.

This is an exhilarating, adventurous ride that will appeal to more seasoned mountain bikers. At times this route is almost spooky. The chance of seeing a bear, or at least signs of a bruin, is good in the swamps while a blustery day can be eerie with the wind howling through the trees.

The four loops total 11 miles but this route follows only 9 miles of trail and ends with 2 miles on Hagerman Lake Road and Forest Road 101 to avoid backtracking. The 11-mile ride feels longer than it is due to the rolling topography and the variety of terrain you ride through.

Intermediate bikers will enjoy this route and beginners can endure it if they are prepared to hop off their bike now and then. But families with younger children may want to look elsewhere because of single track sections that are tight and technical and the fact that some portions of the trail are poorly marked.

Getting There: Head west on US-2 from Iron River for a mile then turn south on Lake Ottawa Road (also known as FR-101) for 4 miles to the Lake Ottawa National Forest Campground. Proceed through the campground, following signs for the Ge-Che Trailhead. You can park at the boat launch.

Information: Contact Iron River Ranger District, 999 Lawey Rd., Iron River, MI 49935; ☎ (906) 265-5139.

Ge-Che Trail

Distance: 11 miles
Trail: Single track, two-track and segments of road
Direction: Clockwise

From the parking area head back up the paved road, following the blue diamonds to a large sign announcing the Ge-Che Trail. By beginning with the Bennan Lake Loop first you get the most difficult portion of the trail out of the way while your legs are still fresh. This segment is initially along Lake Ottawa, and in the campground the trail may be confusing. Just remember to keep the lake on your left until reaching a trail map sign at the start of the single track.

The first mile of single track is so tight that your handlebars brush against branches. After a quick uphill you'll traverse a rocky ridge and then descend with an off-camber downhill. At the bottom of the hill make a left to continue onto the Bennan Lake loop. The trail alternately narrows then widens and features plenty of deadfall and rocks that will keep you concentrating on the path.

You enter a rolling hardwood forest along some sweet single track with curves, twists, dipsy-doodles, compressed rollers and rocks. The downhills appear almost imperceptible but are deceptively fast and will carry you a long way. Just beyond

Mile 2 the trail descends for a nice view of Bennan Lake. A quarter mile later you'll come to a post that signifies the cut-off spur back to FR-101. Continue on.

Directional signposts at *Mile 2.7* mark the north end of the Ge-Che Loop, which begins with a climb up a rocky ridge. This ridge then will deposit you at the back end of a wastewater treatment area. Stay to the left around the plant, and make a left on a two-track road that has been gated to motorized users.

Make another left onto a dirt road for a short distance and a mild climb, then hang a right along a single track with barrier posts in the middle of the trail. This junction is unmarked and may be confusing.

A spur to Hagerman Lake is passed at *Mile 3.8* and then the trail opens up in a stretch where its easy to get your cruising speed up. After a nifty little downhill veer right and keep a close eye on the trail as it is hard to follow here until you reach the posted intersection at *Mile 4.5*.

The arrow at the junction points left to the rest of the trail system at Covenant Point. But the first half mile follows a powerline route though the middle of a swamp that makes for wet and miserable riding. A much better route is to continue to FR-101 then head south on it for less than a mile. The wetlands you pass is a testament to the low terrain you're traversing. Return to the trail at a well-marked entrance on the right side of FR-101 at *Mile 5.2*.

The trail begins as a wide path through a stand of pines but at Mile 6 becomes more rugged with overgrown grass and strewn rocks. After crossing FR-101 you reach the posted junction to Loggers Loop at *Mile 7.3*. Head right. Within a quarter mile the route becomes hilly in a hardwood forest with lots of deadfall.

Near *Mile 8* is a posted junction with one arrow pointing south to the bottom half of Loggers Loop, an extremely overgrown and wet segment. For a much more pleasant (and drier)

Mountain Biking Michigan

ride, turn left instead to climb the hill found on this crossover spur. At the top make a left at the posted junction and then enjoy the downhill run that begins with a yellow cautionary sign for cross country skiers. Have fun but be aware of the tree roots, rocks, and deadfall that can quickly undermine any downhill effort.

At **Mile 9** you enter a meadow and just past it is the southern trailhead near Covenant Point Bible Camp on Hagerman Lake Road. The final leg of this ride is 2 miles of dirt road. First head left (west) on Hagerman Lake Road and then right (north) on FR-101 to return to your vehicle.

180

Land 'O Lakes Rail-Trail

County: Gogebic
Total Mileage: 8 miles
Terrain: Forested areas, wetlands and Duck Creek
Fees: None
Difficulty: Easy

The Watersmeet/Land O' Lakes Trail is a nice, easy jaunt through the lake-studded backcountry of the western U.P. It's a good afternoon activity in a long weekend or even a week spent enjoying the many other recreation areas in this region of the state.

Tops among them is Sylvania Wilderness, a 21,000-acre playground for anglers, canoers, backpackers and backcountry campers. Mountain bike opportunities also abound in this area and include the Pomeroy/Henry Lake and Ehlco Mountain Bike Complexes.

This ride is along a flat rail trail of crushed gravel and some sand that follows Duck Creek and passes through stands of virgin-like pines, swamps, marshes with beaver lodges and across several small bridges. The trail actually begins at a junction with the State Line Trail on the west side of Star Route 45 at the north end of the town of Watersmeet. But I found it was easier to pick it up where US-2 passes over it a half mile south.

For a more extended ride or even a multiple-day adventure, pack along some camping equipment and combine this trail with the State Line Trail and the Little Falls Trail.

Getting There: It's best to park at the Watersmeet Visitor Center for the Ottawa National Forest at US-2 and US-45 and head east 300 yards on US-2 to the overpass. The overpass was originally built to carry traffic over the railroad. Now it does the same for the rail trail. Once on the trail, head south.

Information: Contact the Ottawa National Forest, P.O. Box 276, Watersmeet, MI 49969; ☎ (906) 358-4551.

Watersmeet/Land O' Lakes Trail
Distance: 16 miles roundtrip
Trail: Rail trail

Portions of this trail are multiple use, and near Watersmeet you may encounter ATV tracks. Like all things in the U.P., however, other users are few and far between. Even though ATV's share the trail the surface is in good condition in most areas.

At **Mile 1.6** the terrain opens up to your first glimpse of several wetlands the trail traverses. From here the trail surface alternates between sandy hardpack and crushed gravel, and hardwood and pine forests. These wetland and marshy areas are home to many kinds of wildlife, including herons, and a lot of fragrant natural aromas. Pack along a pair of compact binoculars and take time to search these areas to spot wildlife.

Like many rail trails, this one does not offer a lot of terrain changing and geographic extremes, but it's a nice leisurely jaunt for those out for an easy afternoon. For the next 4 miles you pedal through classical U.P. forest with several small bridges over wetlands areas and Duck Creek. At **Mile 5.2** the trail stabs through one of the more scenic swampy areas, and between **Mile 7.3** and **Mile 7.7** the surface becomes rather sandy.

The trail ends at the Land O' Lakes Library in Land O' Lakes, Wisconsin, a hamlet that provides you with sundry stores or lunch stops. Backtrack when you're ready to return.

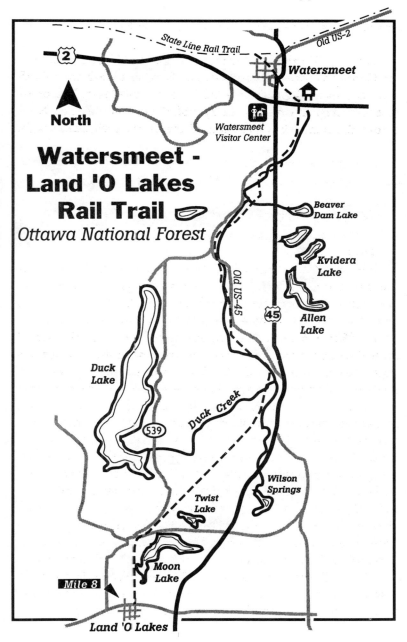

**Watersmeet -
Land 'O Lakes
Rail Trail**
Ottawa National Forest

North

State Line Rail Trail

Old US-2

Watersmeet

Watersmeet
Visitor Center

Beaver
Dam Lake

Kvidera
Lake

Allen
Lake

Old US-45

Duck
Lake

Duck Creek

Wilson
Springs

Twist
Lake

Moon
Lake

Mile 8

Land 'O Lakes

The highlight of the ride along the Little Falls Rail Trail is viewing Bond Falls at the north end.

Little Falls
Rail Trail

Counties: Ontonagon and Gogebic
Total Mileage: 12 miles
Terrain: Mature forests, wetlands, Bond Falls
Fees: None
Difficulty: Moderate

The Little Falls Trail is an excellent ride for wetlands lovers and wildlife watchers. This abandoned railway weaves through numerous swamps and marshes before emptying you onto Bond Falls Road and the Bond Falls Flowage Recreation Area.

The flowage, a 2,200-acre impoundment, is owned by the Upper Peninsula Power Company, which maintains campsites, boat ramps, foot trails, picnic areas, and a general store. The flowage provides electricity to a significant portion of the U.P.

Created in 1937 when the Middle Branch of the Ontonagon River and three feeder streams were dammed, Bond Falls Flowage is an angler's haven, known to have produced a lunker 33-pound Northern Pike and 41-pound Muskie. Where the dam ends, Bond Falls begins, a 50-foot cascade that many consider second only to Tahquamenon Falls for the spectacular beauty of its tumbling water.

Getting There: The southern trailhead is 3 miles east of Watersmeet. From Watersmeet, head north on US-45 and then east on Old US-2. Turn north on Buck Lake Road past Perch Lake to where the trail crosses the road heading west and is distinguished by orange blazes. Stop signs, set up by snowmobilers, face the trail. In the other direction to the south it is easy to jump onto the State Line Rail Trail and head west to Watersmeet. In fact, you will cross over the trail when you turn onto Buck Lake Road.

Information: Contact the Ottawa National Forest, P.O. Box 276, Watersmeet, MI 49969; ☎ (906) 358-4551.

Little Falls Rail Trail

Distance: 12 miles one way
Trail: Rail trail with some ties and sand

Trains used to weave their way through this portion of the Ottawa National Forest, and that fact is hard to believe. Often one thinks of rail trails as semi-paved 'super' trails.

Not this one. This old railway gets pretty rugged in places, and the intact railroad ties offer a challenging change of pace, literally.

The trail actually begins at the State Line Trail just off Old US-2, but I found it far easier to begin the ride off Buck Lake Road, primarily because there is no place to park to the south. From Buck Lake Road, the trail immediately comes to Buck Lake, which is home to a pair of bald eagles that make their nest above the trail. You have to veer to the right at about **Mile 0.8** and follow the blue blazes. Between **Mile 1.6** and **Mile 2.3** the railroad ties have been left in place. This makes for a very bumpy ride that seems longer than it actually is (I walked it on the way back). Mercifully the railroad ties disappear, but get those legs pumping to try and defeat the sand trap that awaits you.

At this point there are almost continuous wetlands on one

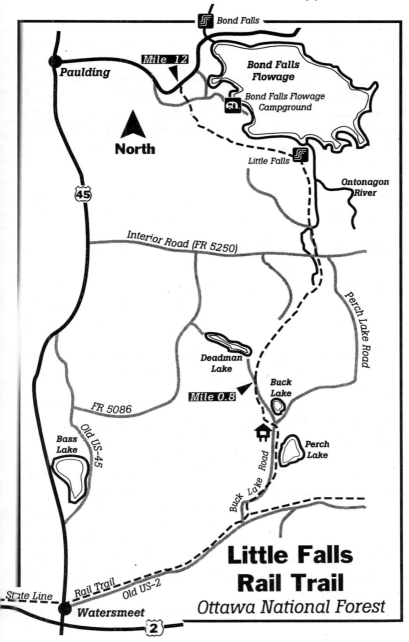

Bond Falls

Mile 12

Paulding

North

45

Interior Road (FR 5250)

**Bond Falls
Flowage**

60

Bond Falls Flowage
Campground

Little Falls

**Ontonagon
River**

Perch Lake Road

Deadman
Lake

Mile 0.8

**Buck
Lake**

FR 5086

Old US-45

**Bass
Lake**

Buck Lake Road

**Perch
Lake**

State Line

Rail Trail

Old US-2

Watersmeet

2

Little Falls
Rail Trail
Ottawa National Forest

side or the other, and often both. This is adventurous mountain biking but it's really easy to know how close you are to wildlife - you can hear the deer splashing ahead as you pedal through this deep forest experience. At **Mile 4.4** the trail turns into a logging road, and at **Mile 5.3** it turns into a sandy hardpack. The trail then winds through the forest on this logging road, and it is difficult to believe full-sized railroad cars actually fit through here.

The logging road carves its way past the wee Little Falls, and melds into the Bond Falls Flowage campground, and eventually to Bond Falls Road at **Mile 12**. One word of caution - the UPPC has an active logging operation in the area that constantly uses the logging roads.

Bond Falls Flowage is a recreational facility managed by UPPC and includes 48 rustic campsites spread around the 2,200-acre lake. Campsites are secured on a first-come-first-served basis. No reservations accepted. Bond Falls is located just east of the campground entrance off Bond Falls Road and reached with a half-mile hike that includes numerous stairways. The falls, actually a series of cascades, are stunning and well worth the extra time to walk to them.

An interesting side trip for history buffs is the Barclay Cemetery in the campground. It contains 11 graves of young people, most of whom died from typhoid fever in the spring of 1902.

Watersmeet Ski Trails

County: Gogebic
Total Mileage: 10 miles
Terrain: Ridgelines, rolling forested hills, marshes
Fees: None
Difficulty: Moderate

In cooperation with the Ottawa National Forest, Sylvania Outfitters, Inc. maintains a 10-mile-plus trail system for cross country skiers just west of Watersmeet. During the summer, the outfitters allow, but don't promote, mountain biking on the trails.

The terrain is interesting and there are some scenic spots, particularly Rickles Lake. But keep in mind that trails, a mix of two-track and single track, are not maintained for off-road cycling and the use is light. Some sections will be too overgrown to be enjoyable by all but hard-core bikers. Also be aware that the marshes and wetlands are a haven for bug production. There's lots of skeeters in these woods.

This route describes the main loops to Pilot Lake with a side trip to Rickles Lake, a ride of 6.8 miles. At Sylvania Outfitters, which doubles as the trailhead, you can purchase snacks and amenities or even come back the next day and arrange a canoe trip.

Getting There: From Watersmeet, head west on US-2 to Sylvania Outfitters, reached in a little more than a mile.

Information: Contact Sylvania Outfitters, West US-2, Watersmeet, MI 49969; ☎ (906) 358-4766.

Pilot Loop

Distance: 6.8 miles
Trail: Single track and two-track
Direction: Clockwise

Begin under the *Ski Trail* sign on the west side of the outfitter's shop. The first half mile is a cornucopia of trail signs and junctions. You pass five of them in this short segment, including Dog Leg and Woof loops. Keep heading straight toward Post 4, easy to find as it is the most natural route and there are trail maps at every junction.

After Post 2D, the trail begins to roll and includes an occasional skier's bypass. Post 4 is reached just before **Mile 1**, where you veer right, then left to quickly encounter a couple of steep downhills and ensuing climbs. There are a few other two-tracks here but blue diamonds clearly show the way to Post 6. You follow a low ridge with open marshes on both sides and reach the junction at the top of Deer Trail Loop at **Mile 1.5**.

At Post 6, the trail changes from a wide path to a true two-track and the riding becomes considerably easier. You enjoy a couple of fun downhills and reach Post 8 and the Hemlock Loop near **Mile 2**. There is a *Do Not Enter* sign for skiers at this side of the Hemlock Loop but mountain bikers can continue following the two-track over the rolling terrain to Post 11 at the bottom of Danger Hill. Located here is a gorgeous stream featuring several beaver dams. After you admire that beauty,

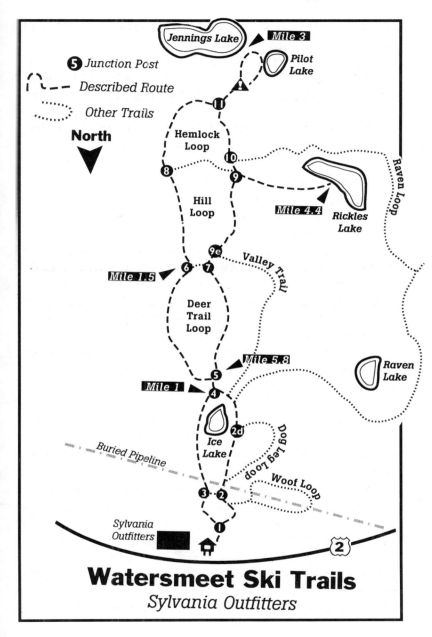

Watersmeet Ski Trails
Sylvania Outfitters

Jennings Lake

Mile 3

Pilot
Lake

5 *Junction Post*

Described Route

Other Trails

North

Hemlock
Loop

Hill
Loop

Raven Loop

Mile 4.4

Rickles
Lake

Valley Trail

Mile 1.5

Deer
Trail
Loop

Raven
Lake

Mile 5.8

Mile 1

Buried Pipeline

Ice
Lake

Dog Leg Loop

Woof Loop

Sylvania
Outfitters

feast your eyes on the climb just ahead, then shift into your granny gear. Did you make it? Well, better luck next time.

At 1,770 feet, Danger Hill is a 160 feet higher than the trailhead, making the return trip easier. Continue south, however, to view peaceful Jennings Lake, reached near **Mile 3**, before returning to Post 11 and heading toward Post 9 along a two-track.

At Post 9, a two-track swings west and ends at Rickles Lake, a one-way ride of less than a half mile. The sidetrip is worth it as you can sit on a shaded bank and take in the beauty of this scenic body of water. Backtrack to Post 9, reached at **Mile 4.8**, and this time continue north along a single track marked by blue diamonds.

It's a rapid downhill to Post 9E at the edge of open meadow. A two-track jogs right to Post 7 and then it's back to single track for the last time to reach Post 5 at **Mile 5.8**. This is a hilly stretch along a rough trail.

You return to two-track at Post 5 and veer right to continue to Post 3 and eventually the trailhead next to the shop. The final mile is wide and level for an easy finish.

Henry Lake & Pomeroy Lake

Mountain Bike Complex

County: Gogebic
Total Mileage: 86 miles
Terrain: Rolling forests and lakes
Fees: None
Difficulty: Easy to moderate

The Henry and Pomeroy Lake Mountain Bike Complex is a vast system of forest roads in the lake-studded region of the Ottawa National Forest along the Michigan/Wisconsin border. The U.S. Forest Service posted the 86-mile network in 1994 in response to the increasing number of "where can we ride" inquires it was receiving from mountain bikers.

Part of the Mines and Pines Mountain Bike Trail System that spreads across western U.P. and into Wisconsin's Iron County, Henry and Pomeroy Lake was purposely set up for novice off-road cyclists and families. There are no twisty singly tracks here or beaver dams to tiptoe across as encountered in the Ehlco Mountain Bike Complex. All the routes are laid out on either gravel forest roads or the State Line Rail-Trail, which resembles a two-track.

You could ride most of the system on a road bike but it

would be laborious at best. A hybrid is better choice and a true mountain bike would provide the easiest trip of all.

The system is located south of the town of Marenisco and split by M-65. On the west half is the 22.8-mile Henry Lake portion; on the east the 63-mile network around Pomeroy Lake. The State Line Rail-Trail crosses M-64 to connect the two halves. The routes are well posted by a blue mountain biker symbol and easy to follow.

The number of different loops you can ride in this complex are almost limitless. Described here are two routes, one from each half, that includes the best scenery the area has to offer. They both begin at a national forest campground and make an excellent destination for a weekend combining mountain biking with camping and fishing.

Getting There: Marenisco is 26 miles west of Watersmeet. To reach Henry Lake Campground, turn off US-2 onto Old US-2, and follow it west 4 miles to Forest Road-8100. Turn south on FR-8100 to reach the campground in 5 miles.

To reach Pomeroy Lake Campground, turn onto FR-7300 from US-2 4 miles east of Marenisco. FR-7300 reaches the national forest campground in 10 miles.

Information: Contact the Forest Supervisor's Office, Ottawa National Forest, Ironwood, MI 49938; ☎ (906) 932-1330.

Henry Lake Loop
Distance: 11 miles
Trail: Gravel roads
Direction: Counter clockwise

This is an easy 11-mile ride along gravel roads that takes you past or near eight lakes. If riding with children, pack along a lunch and plan an extended break at a boat launch on one of them. You can begin this loop from either the Teal Canoe Landing parking lot on the south side of the bridge across the West

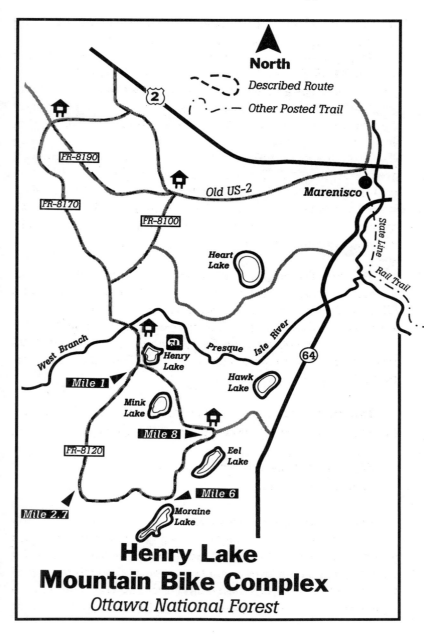

North

- - - - **Described Route**
- · - · - **Other Posted Trail**

2

Old US-2

Marenisco

State Line

Rail Trail

FR-8190

FR-8170

FR-8100

Heart Lake

West Branch

Presque Isle River

64

Henry Lake

Hawk Lake

Mile 1

Mink Lake

Mile 8

Eel Lake

FR-8120

Mile 6

Mile 2.7

Moraine Lake

Henry Lake
Mountain Bike Complex
Ottawa National Forest

A group of bikers pause at one of the many lakes within the Henry Lake Mountain Bike Complex in the Ottawa National Forest.

Branch of the Presque Isle River, or from Henry Lake Campground further south along FR-8100.

From the canoe landing you pass the entrance to the campground in a third of a mile. Henry Lake is a small and pleasant campground. Of the 11 sites, five of them are on a low rise overlooking the lake. Other amenities include a boat launch and a large T-shaped fishing pier. FR-8100 continues south of the campground entrance and reaches a junction with FR-8120 near **Mile 1**. Veer right onto FR-8120.

At **Mile 1.3**, you pass the entrance to the boat launch on

Thrust Lake and in another mile pass a small lake to the west. If riding in the early morning or evening, stop here to search for wildlife. At *Mile 2.7* FR-8120 narrows to a single lane and swings sharply east while an old two-track continues south. Blue mountain bike symbols will keep you on FR-8120.

The scenery remains an unbroken forest until *Mile 5.5*, when you cross Moraine Creek. The entrance to the boat launch on Moraine Lake is reached at *Mile 6* and makes an excellent place for a lunch stop. The gravel road becomes more hilly after the lake, swings north and at *Mile 7.4* reaches the half-mile entrance road to scenic Eel Lake.

Continuing north, you arrive at the junction with FR-8100 just before *Mile 8*. Turn left (west) and at *Mile 9.3* you will pass the north end of Mink Lake, a large body of water. Bluejay and Orchid lakes immediately follow on the north side of the road, and near *Mile 10* you return to the junction of FR-8120 and FR-8100. Turn right and the canoe landing will be reached in another mile.

Pomeroy Lake Loop

Distance: 24 miles
Trail: Gravel roads and rail-trail
Direction: Counter clockwise

This 24-mile route begins and ends at the Pomeroy Campground and is rated moderate due to its length and a long climb on FR-7300. More than a third of the route follows the State Line Rail-Trail which allows you to stay dry despite passing through an interesting swamp.

If not camping at Pomeroy Lake, then park in the small lot at the boat launch. Begin the ride by following the campground entrance road for almost a mile to a stop sign at Pomeroy Lake Road (also labeled as County Road-525). Turn right.

The next 2 miles are a level ride through the forest until you reach a junction with FR-7100 (still CR-525 on maps) at *Mile 2.8*. Turn right to follow Langford Lake Road (also labeled

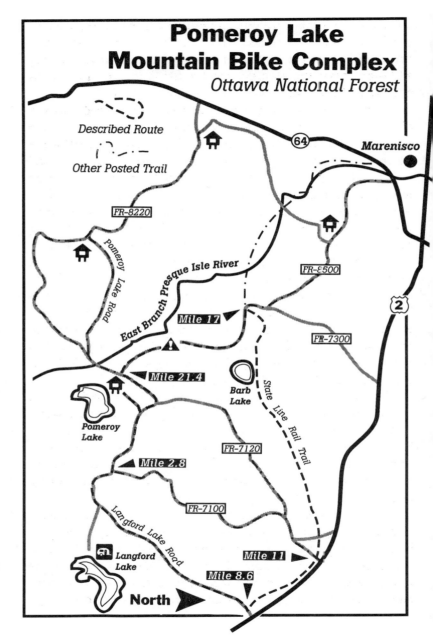

CR-527). Both FR-7100 and Langford Lake Road will lead to the State Line Rail-Trail, but the latter is much more scenic. It begins by crossing a single lane bridge over Tenderfoot Creek and then passes the entrance road to the Langford Lake Campground at *Mile 3.8*.

The gravel road then enters a dense forest, so dense and thick in places that the trees form a foliage tunnel at times and keep you cool even on the hottest day in August. At *Mile 8.6* you arrive at a stop sign on Old US-2, a paved road. Turn left to immediately reach the State Line Rail Trail that is posted with mountain bike symbols on the south side. The rail-trail quickly crosses Grosbeck Creek and then heads northwest, paralleling Old US-2 for most the next 2 miles. After crossing Tenderfoot Creek you reach FR-7100 at *Mile 11*.

Stay on the rail-trail for one of the most interesting stretches of the entire complex as it passes through a vast wetland. It's a 6-mile ride before you reach the next posted forest road and in the first half the rail-trail passes through a swamp and crosses Santa Fe and Slate creeks. The trail then swings more to the south and skirts Barb and Benner lakes before emerging at FR-7300 at *Mile 17*. If you stayed on the State Line Rail-Trail you would eventually reach Marenisco.

This route, however, departs from it and heads left (south) on FR-7300. Within a mile on the wide gravel road you pass a small pond and at *Mile 18.8* begin climbing steadily. This climb lasts for more than a mile but near the top is a posted scenic area. Here a bench has been built overlooking the East Branch of the Presque Isle River, where several beavers have set up house. Take a break. You deserve it after that climb.

The road soon tops off after the scenic overlook and arrives at a stop sign at *Mile 21.4*. Turn left on Pomeroy Lake Road. You'll pass the posted Bluebill Creek Grouse Management Area in 1.5 miles and arrive at the entrance to the Pomeroy Lake Campground just beyond *Mile 27*. Turn right and the end of the ride and your car is less than a mile away.

Copper Harbor Pathway includes a 2-mile segment along the south shore of Lake Fanny Hooe.

Copper Harbor Pathway

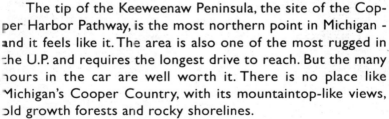

County: Keweenaw
Total Mileage: 12 miles
Terrain: Old-growth forest and lake views
Fees: None
Difficulty: Moderate to strenuous

The tip of the Keeweenaw Peninsula, the site of the Copper Harbor Pathway, is the most northern point in Michigan - and it feels like it. The area is also one of the most rugged in the U.P. and requires the longest drive to reach. But the many hours in the car are well worth it. There is no place like Michigan's Cooper Country, with its mountaintop-like views, old growth forests and rocky shorelines.

Most of these attributes can be experienced and felt on a mountain bike along the Cooper Harbor Pathway, a 12-mile trail system located on the south side of Lake Fanny Hooe. The pathway, designed as a cross country ski trail, is a series of six loops, of which only Green Trail, Kamakazie Loop and Clark Mine Loop are of interest to mountain bikers. This 9-mile route is a combination of the three plus an opportunity to drop your bike and hike an additional mile to view the old growth trees within Estivant Pines Sanctuary, where biking is prohibited.

As long as you've driven so far to get here, take time to enjoy the many one-blinker towns, abandoned copper mines and spectacular shoreline scenery. A great way to do that is on a bike following one of the many road trips described in the road route sections of this guide (see page 271).

Getting There: From either M-26 or US-41 head east into Copper Harbor. Turn right at the Lake Fanny Hooe Resort and the trailhead and parking area will be reached near the west end of the lake.

Information: Contact Fort Wilkins State Park, P.O. Box 71, Copper Harbor, MI 49918; ☎ (906) 289-4215.

Copper Harbor Pathway
Distance: 9 miles
Trail: Single track and dirt road
Direction: Clockwise

Start at Post I just past the motor lodge, and at a half mile in is a stream crossing with a partial bridge. The crossing is easy, the terrain that follows rugged. I mean rugged. I chose to head clockwise to get this gnarly section out of the way first and to enjoy a long downhill at the end of the route. The reverse direction, counter-clockwise, allows you to avoid some of the uphills.

The section along Lake Fanny Hooe of the Kamakazie Loop contains nonstop, moss-covered rocks, tree roots and huge, droopy pines. *Be careful along this stretch, or walk it if you're uncomfortable.* The rocks get bigger, allowing technical riders to play the Artful Dodger when choosing a line on the trail.

At **Mile 1.6** the trail rises away from the lake and loses some of its rocky disposition. The forest also changes to more mixed hardwood. You can still see the lake, but eventually it shrinks away as you climb the ridge. At **Mile 2.5** there are a pair of tricky log crossings followed by a steep uphill and two

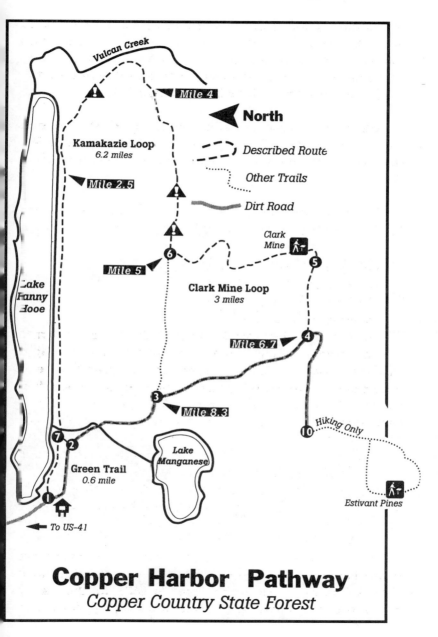

Vulcan Creek

⚠

Mile 4

◄ **North**

Kamakazie Loop
6.2 miles

---) Described Route

.... Other Trails

~~~ Dirt Road

Mile 2.5

⚠

Clark
Mine 🚶

⚠

Mile 5

6

5

Clark Mine Loop
3 miles

Lake
Fanny
Hooe

Mile 6.7

4

3

Mile 8.3

10 Hiking Only

7

2

Lake
Manganese

Green Trail
0.6 mile

🏕

Estivant Pines

1

🏠

◄ To US–41

Copper Harbor Pathway
Copper Country State Forest

of its little sisters. The grind is worth it. At the top you look down and realize you are on a solid rock bluff that provides a 360-degree view of the area. This is an excellent spot to de-mount, do a little exploring, or catch your breath.

Near **Mile 4** you begin descending the back side of the ridge, moving into a forest of mixed hardwoods again. You en-counter some significant climbs while passing a sheer bluff on the right. The timber here is tall and at times the late after-noon sun can make it a little spooky. At **Mile 5** is the junction for the Clark Mine Loop; head left to enjoy a nice little down-hill. Beware of the wet area at the bottom that can be very wet after a recent rain.

More water in the form of a small pond is reached at **Mile 6**. Luckily, there are rocks on which you can walk around in an effort to keep your feet dry. An uphill later the trail reaches Clark Mine. Incorporated in 1853, Clark Mine reached its peak production in 1858 when it yielded 187,915 pounds of copper.

At **Mile 6.7** is the junction to the Estivant Pines. To see these stunning old-growth trees you need to head left and ride to a parking lot and posted entrance for the Estivant Pines Sanctuary. Leave the bike behind and continue left from the parking lot as this section of the pathway is for foot traffic only.

The stand of giant white pines was named for Edouard Estivant, a Frenchman who purchased the tract in the 1870s. The parcel changed hands a couple of times and was scheduled for logging in 1970 when the Michigan Nature Association staged a series of fund raisers to purchase the tract and saved the trees. From the parking lot the Memorial Loop is a 1.2-mile walk into two stands of old growth. Departing off the trail is the mile-long Cathedral Loop into another stand.

Back on Clark Mine Loop head left (north) and follow the dirt road north for basically one long descent back to the trailhead. At **Mile 8.3** you pass the junction where the Kamakazie Loop merges into the road and then come to a spot where you can view most of Lake Fanny Hooe. The trailhead is less than a mile along the road.

Maasto Hiihto Ski Trail

County: Houghton
Total Mileage: 11 miles
Terrain: Hills, meadows, stream crossings, vistas
Fees: None
Difficulty: Easy to strenuous

Maasto Hiihto Ski Trail is in the heart of the Keweenaw Peninsula sandwiched between two of the most traditional U.P. towns you will find - Houghton and Hancock. Houghton, home of Michigan Tech University, is to the east on one side of Portage Canal. Hancock borders the 11-mile trail system to the south.

The land that Maasto Hiihto winds through has a variety of uses; a cross country ski trail, snowmobile trail, an old garbage dump and an abandoned mine. The system is composed of six loops that can be a challenge to follow at times, but it's hard to get totally lost here, being so close to Hancock. The easiest ride and the easiest loops to follow are St. Urho's and Quincy, which can be combined for a 3-mile route.

Below is a brief description of each loop. The best way to enjoy this area is pack a compass, know your boundary roads, and not worry too much where you are. Just have fun and you'll eventually make it back to your car.

Getting There: There are three trailheads with parking to Maasto Hiihto. The western trailhead is off M-203 behind the Eagles Club north of Hancock. The eastern trailheads are at end of Poplar Street off Ingot Street and behind the Houghton County Arena off Birch Street. Both eastern trailheads are reached by following US-41 north through Hancock and watching for signs.

Information: The best place for additional information is Keweenaw Tourism Council, P.O.. Box 336, Calumet, MI 49913; ☎ (800) 338-7982; or Cross Country Sports, 507 Oak St., Calumet, MI 49913; ☎ (906) 337-4520.

Maasto Hiihto Ski Trail

Trail: Two-track, single track and gravel road

The best place to start is the trailhead behind the Houghton County Arena, where signs for cross-country skiers direct you to head right (east) along the *St. Urho's Loop*. This loop heads northeast to the Quincy Loop, and is characterized partially by a tree-canopied trail and partly by wide open meadows.

On the *Quincy Loop* the trail then winds behind a church and the Cypress Manor. The St. Urho's and Quincy loops can be combined for an easy, 3-mile ride through flat land and along gravel roads.

The Quincy Loop will also lead you to a large intersection, where you can head right into Railroad Ravine and the meat of the trail system. It's a sharp drop into the ravine that was once used by railroad cars and now by snowmobilers in the winter. The riding is considerably more difficult along the rest of the trail system and the climb out of the ravine on the other side will be your introduction. At the top, trail markers take you to the right (north) onto Gorge Loop and up the appropriately named Dam Hill.

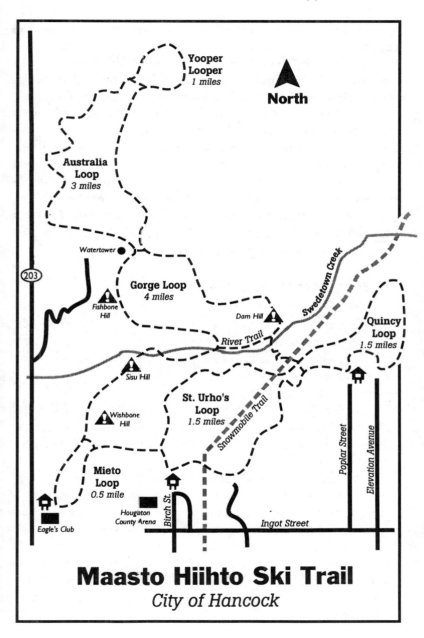

Maasto Hiihto Ski Trail
City of Hancock

Gorge Loop is the longest at 4 miles and here the trail gets a lot rockier as it winds through a mature forest. A highlight of this loop is Sidewinder Pass, a ribbon of trail halfway up one of the hills on the south side of the loop that provides an extensive view. There are some serious hills or this loop, and the gentle pedal along Sidewinder Pass at the end of it is a welcome stretch of trail.

The 2.2-mile **Australia Loop** is reached on the northern side of Gorge Loop, and you enter it with a hairy downhill onto a rough-and-tumble single track. This loop also is characterized by mature forest, but is flatter than Gorge Loop.

The mile-long **Yooper Looper** is the most minimal stretch of trail in the system, with flat, hard-packed sections that give you the feeling of leading you into no man's land. This loop is also a welcome change from the hills encountered in the Australia and Gorge loops. Much of the terrain here is scrub forest that at times brushes against your arms.

The half-mile **Mieto Loop**, on the southern end of the trail system, is characterized by a gravel pit which you wind through before skirting a bubbling stream with a small falls. You end up crossing the stream several times but there are bridges to help you out. This is a beautiful stretch of the trail and if the rest of the loops have worn you out you will want to stop and soak your toes off one of the bridges.

Ehlco
Mountain Bike Complex

County: Ontonagon
Total Mileage: 35 miles
Terrain: Northern hardwood forests, unbridged streams and beavers dams
Fees: None
Difficulty: Strenuous

The Ehlco Mountain Bike Complex is an adventurous ride along gravel roads, overgrown logging roads and trails. The terrain is generally flat but the trip is a challenging one due to numerous beaver dams constantly flooding out the route and unbridged creeks and streams that must be forded. As the U.S. Forest Service says in its description of the trail: Plan on getting wet and muddy!

The trailhead is on the south side of Porcupine Mountain Wilderness State Park but the vast majority of the system lies in Ottawa National Forest. Most of the trail is gravel roads and old logging two-tracks that are 4- to 14-feet-wide and marked by blue mountain biker signs. But don't underestimate this ride due to the lack of technical single track. Pack along a compass, water, parka and some high-energy food (i.e. candy) just in case you get turned around and have to spend more time in the woods than planned.

This route follows the perimeter of the system and includes fording the West Branch of the Big Iron River just before its confluence with the main stream. There is no bridge at this crossing and in the spring or after a particularly hard rain, the stream may be difficult if not impossible to cross. It's wise to check for conditions prior to embarking on your ride by calling the Bergland Ranger District office.

If a 27-mile day is too much than use the cutoff spur along Forest Road 366 to ride just the west end of the trail system. This makes for a 12-mile loop that avoids the most challenging segment of the trail, including the West Branch ford.

Getting There: From Silver City head west on M-107 to Porcupine Mountains Wilderness State Park and then south on South Boundary Road. Follow the park road to Summit Peak Road. The trail begins at the intersection and parking is available just up Summit Peak Road. The trail can also be picked up 6 miles north of Bergland at M-64 and Forest Road 360.

Information: Contact the Bergland Ranger District, Bergland, MI 49910; ☎ (906) 575-3441.

Ehlco Mountain Bike Complex

Distance: 27 miles
Trail: Gravel roads and two-track
Direction: Clockwise

From Summit Peak Road head left (northeast) on South Boundary Road to begin the trip in the Porcupine Mountains Wilderness State Park. Just past **Mile 1**, veer right onto a gravel logging road that is gated closed and unmarked. Within a half mile the first of many beaver ponds will be encountered. These are adjacent to the trail but don't be surprised if they have flooded the route.

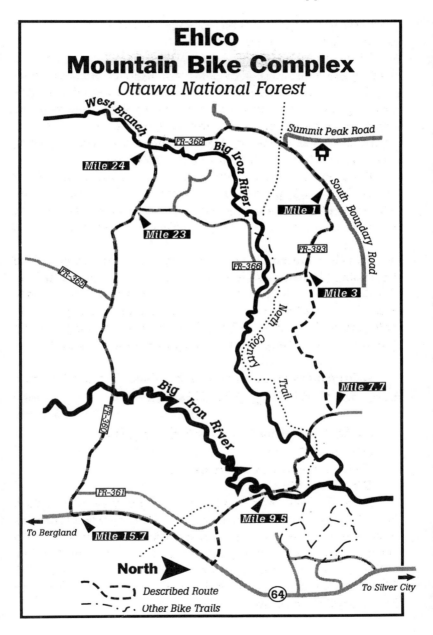

Ehlco
Mountain Bike Complex
Ottawa National Forest

West Branch

FR-368

Big Iron River

Summit Peak Road

Mile 24

Mile 23

South Boundary Road

Mile 1

FR-393

FR-366

FR-365

Mile 3

North Country Trail

Mile 7.7

Big Iron River

FR-360

FR-361

Mile 9.5

To Bergland

Mile 15.7

North

Described Route

Other Bike Trails

64

To Silver City

At **Mile 3** head left (east) at a junction onto a rough, dirt logging road. For almost the next 4 miles you'll follow this overgrown two-track through the most remote section of the tract, a forest of northern hardwoods, aspen and white pine. Be prepared to navigate several stream crossings and beaver ponds, but also take time to stop and study the ponds for possible wildlife.

You arrive at FR-361 at **Mile 7.7**. Turn right (south) and in less than a mile you will arrive at the West Branch of the Big Iron River for the first time. You must ford the stream as there is no bridge and should do it cautiously during periods of high water. Once across, the most challenging segment of the route is behind you.

FR-361 is a cleared logging road that reaches the main branch of the Big Iron River at **Mile 9.5**. Thanks to the North Country National Scenic Trail, a bridge has been built across the river. On the other side is the access road that was used to build the bridge and now makes for easy riding for the next 2 miles. Eventually the posted route leaves FR-361 and follows a half mile of rough trail to reached paved M-64 at **Mile 12.3**.

Turn right on the state highway and follow the paved shoulder south for 3.4 miles to the junction of FR-360, reached at **Mile 15.7**. This forest road heads west as an open, gravel logging road that may have considerable traffic in the form of large logging trucks. That can be unnerving when they rumble past you but on the other hand the gravel road is free of the beaver ponds and brush encountered in the first half of the trail.

Near **Mile 23** is the junction with FR-366, a cutoff spur that reaches FR-393 in 5 miles. The perimeter route continues west on FR-360, reaching the West Branch of the Big Iron River for the second time at **Mile 24**. The stream is considerably smaller here and can be crossed any time during the biking season. Turn right (north) on FR-368 and be prepared to get your feet wet crossing up to a half dozen ponds in the next mile or so. FR-368 returns you to South Boundary Road at

Mile 25.7. The final leg of the ride is following paved South Boundary Road east for 1.2 miles to Summit Peak Road.

At times, mountain biking the Big Hemlock Ski Trail in the Porcupine Mountains Wilderness State Park can be a wet experience.

Porcupine Mountains

Wilderness State Park

County: Ontonagon
Total Mileage: 23 miles
Terrain: Rocky cliffs, old growth forests, waterfalls
Fees: Vehicle entry permit or annual state park pass
Difficulty: Easy to strenuous

Porcupine Mountains Wilderness State Park offers a rare wilderness setting to mountain bikers along with some of the most challenging and technical riding in area. The rugged park, the largest state park in Michigan at 60,000 acres, is laced with a 90-mile trail system that is open to hikers and backpackers only. But during the summer and fall mountain biking is permitted on the cross-country ski trails, a 23-mile system at the east end of the park.

Affectionally known as "the Porkies," these rugged ridges make for adventure riding for which you need to be prepared. Steep, rocky, uphills and downhills are common, as are numerous water runoff crossings in early and late summer. If it has just rained the moss-covered rocks and tree roots are slick, forcing you into a hike-and-bike adventure. The trails and intersections can be poorly marked at times, so it is best to get a detailed map from the Visitor Center before heading out.

Also keep in mind that this far north, the mountain biking season often doesn't get under way until late May or early June and even then conditions will be sloppy. The best time to ride these trails is July through August. There are numerous trailheads to the cross country trail system but the best place to park in the summer is at the Chalet in Alpine Ski Area, just west of the Union Bay Campground. Pack along plenty of water and high-energy snacks before hitting the trails and once on them figure on doubling your normal riding time.

Is it worth the long drive to the Porkies? You bet, this country is as beautiful as it is rugged and a week spent riding these trails and other systems nearby, like Ehlco Complex, makes for a mountain biking trip that will be hard to surpass anywhere else in Michigan.

Getting There: The east entrance of the park located at the end of M-107, 7 miles from Silver City and 20 miles west of Ontonagon, the largest town in the county. The park's Visitor Center is just south of M-107 on South Boundary Road.

Information: For information on camping in the park or other activities call the park headquarters at ☎ (906) 885-5275. For additional travel information for the region call Western U.P. Convention & Visitor's Bureau at ☎ (906) 932-4850.

Deer Yard and Superior Loop
Distance: 4.5 miles
Trail: Wide pathway
Direction: Counter clockwise

Deer Yard and Superior loops can be combined for a 4.5-mile ride that will be gentle on the mind and easy on the cardiovascular system. This ride begins with the Superior Trail across M-107 from the ski lodge, and takes you toward Lake Superior through a stand of impressive birch. If it has rained recently, there will be a number of puddle crossings because of the low-lying clay soil. A right at the first intersection takes you to the shores of Lake Superior and a right at the next one puts you on Deer Yard loop at *Mile 1*.

This loop gets a little hilly and becomes a cobblestone pathway. Go straight past the turn for the Whitetail Cabin to cross a smallish stream. At *Mile 2.8* into this ride you will venture

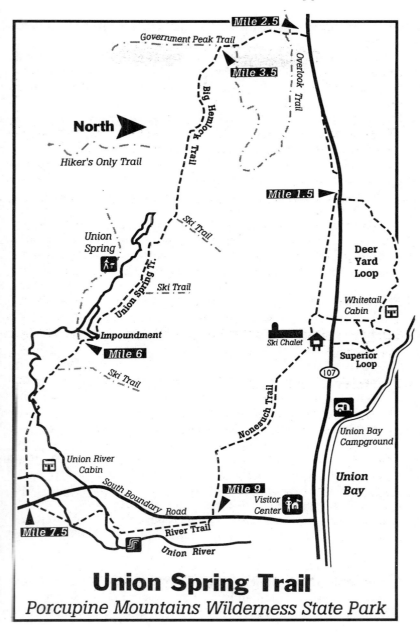

Union Spring Trail
Porcupine Mountains Wilderness State Park

through a towering old-growth hemlock forest. Impressive trees to say the least.

At **Mile 3.2** is a sustained climb to M-107. Cross the paved road and continue the climb until topping out at an intersection. Head left and it's a long downhill run to the ski lodge.

Big Hemlock\Union Spring Trail

Distance: 12 miles
Trail: Wide pathway
Direction: Counter clockwise

This 12-mile ride is a combination of the Big Hemlock, Union Spring, a portion of the River Trail and the Nonesuck Trail. Again, the best place to begin is at the Alpine Ski Area. Head west on Big Hemlock Ski Trail for a gentle ride along a series of small hills. At **Mile 1.5** the trail merges with M-107. Follow the road for about 150 feet and then pick up the trail heading uphill on the south side of M-107. This section, because it is on a hillside, contains a lot of runoff water crossings at times. Further west, the trail returns to the road a second time. At this point follow M-107 to the Government Peak trailhead that is well posted and easy to spot.

Government Peak Trail, reached at **Mile 2.5**, is a hiker's trail that mountain bikers follow for the first mile. This is one of two trail segments in the park that walkers and bikers share. Be conscious of that and when you see hikers or backpackers, stop to let them pass. Also keep in mind that mountain biking is prohibited beyond the junction to the Big Hemlock Ski Trail.

From the trailhead on M-107, you climb steeply into the woods, topping off at a posted junction with the Escarpment Trail heading west and then the Overlook Trail heading east. Continue south along Government Peak Trail and enjoy the downhill run through stands of old growth forests. After crossing a low-lying wet area, turn east just beyond the second junction to the Overlook Trail at **Mile 3.5** to continue with the Big Hemlock Ski Trail.

Mountain bikers are not allowed on the Overlook Trail but instead follow the Big Hemlock Ski Trail as it passes through stands of 300-year-old hemlock and makes a pair of long climbs. The second one tops off at the junction with a ski trail from

West Vista just before **Mile 5**. Stay to the right and enjoy a long downhill road.

The next intersection is reached in less than a half mile. Mountain bikers must stay to the left here and remain on the Union Spring Ski Trail. You are not allowed to ride the hiker's trail to Union Spring itself. The ski trail, an old logging road at this point, reaches the east end of an impoundment near **Mile 6**. Located on the south side of the impoundment is a pair of backcountry campsites and a hiker's only trail to Union Spring, the second largest in the state. The spring is only a half mile to the west and is well worth leaving the bikes and making the short walk to it. There is a floating dock extending out over the pond from which you can view more than 700 gallons of water bubbling out of the ground each minute.

From the impoundment it's 1.5 miles of easy riding along the old logging road to South Boundary Road. Along the way you pass a junction with a ski trail to the East Vista, cross a bridge over the Union River and then pass the spur to the Union River Cabin, one of 16 wilderness cabins you can rent in the park. Keep in mind that from the impoundment to South Boundary Road you are sharing the trail with hikers.

At **Mile 7.5** you emerge in a parking area and then reach South Boundary Road. If you've had enough mountain biking for one day you can follow the pavement north and then head west on M-107 to return to the Chalet. Or you can return via the River Ski Trail.

This trail resumes on the other side of the road with a gentle downhill through the forest. After a pair of climbs you descend to the vehicle bridge across the Union River and then enjoy the most scenic stretches of the route. For the next mile you follow a wide ski path with Union River and its waterfalls on one side and a towering wooded bluff on the other.

South Boundary Road is crossed a second time near **Mile 9** On the other side the trail resumes for the final 3-mile leg of the loop. After crossing Jamison Creek, you arrive at a posted junction. Head right (north) on Nonesuch Trail and it's 1.5 miles back to the parking lot. The final mile includes some knee-bending climbs before you arrive at the Chalet at **Mile 12**.

A challenging ride from Copper Peak Mountain Bike Park is a segment of the North Country Trail that winds north past five waterfalls, including Potawatomi Falls, on its way to Lake Superior.

220

Copper Peak
Mountain Bike Park

County: Gogebic
Total Mileage: 12 miles
Terrain: Ski jumping hill and the Black River
Fees: Trail fee
Difficulty: Strenuous

The most impressive structure in the Upper Peninsula is the Copper Peak Ski Flying Complex, a ramp with so many steel girders it's been dubbed the Yooper Eiffel Tower. Constructed with 300 tons of steel, the 469-foot-long slide towers 421 feet above the summit of Copper Park and is the only ski flying hill in the country. In 1976, Hans-Georg Aschenbach of East Germany, a gold-medal winner at the Winter Olympics, sailed 505 feet off the end of the ramp to set a hill record.

International ski flying tournaments are no longer held at Copper Peak but in the summer and fall you can still ride the chairlift to the base of the ramp and then take an elevator to the top. The view is awesome; a 360-degree panorama that includes Wisconsin, Minnesota and Michigan. If the day is clear you might even see across Lake Superior to Thunder Bay.

As impressive as the view are the downhill opportunities for mountain bikers. The Copper Peak Mountain Bike Park was organized in 1997 and in its first season featured 12 miles of mostly wide ski trails and some single track that departed from the base of the ramp and extended east to the Black River.

For a $10 daily fee you not only have access to the trail system but also unlimited rides on the chairlift that is outfitted with a special bike rack on the back. Near the base of the ski ramp are several trails and a maintenance road that depart from the summit of Copper Peak for the Entrance Road below. One run that winds around the north side of the peak is a wicked descent of 400 feet where downhillers have reached speeds of close to 40 mph. The trails on the south side are not as gonzo-like but all of them are for advanced bikers or people with a good health insurance policy.

East of the Entrance Road are four more loops with one that dips down to the Black River. These 10-foot-wide trails are much more suitable for intermediate bikers. Future plans call for posting another 3 miles of trail, including a spur on this east side that would lead to the Chippewa Waterfalls on the Black River. With the exception of a small loop through a field near the gift shop, all the trails are in the woods.

Also at Copper Peak is the southern trailhead for the Black River Segment of the North Country Trail that parallels the river to Lake Superior. This is a stunning stretch of trail that passes six impressive waterfalls before crossing the Black River on a swing bridge in a national forest campground at Black Harbor. Opened to mountain biking in 1997, this 5-mile stretch of the NCT makes for a very challenging and technical ride along tight single track. The trailhead is near the north end of the Entrance Road where it returns to County Road 513.

Getting There: From US-2 in Bessemer, head north on County Road 513, also labeled Black River Drive. Within 10 miles you will reach the posted entrance to Copper Peak.

Information: Contact the Copper Peak Mountain Bike Park at ☎ (906) 932-3857 or ☎ (800) 222-3131 or the Hobby Wheel Bike Shop in Ironwood at ☎ (906) 932-3332.

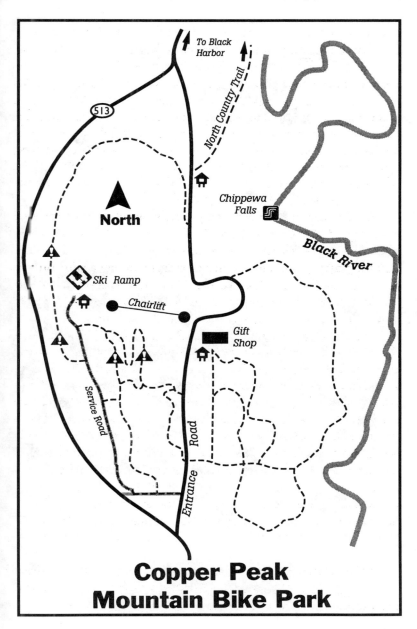

513

To Black
Harbor

North County Trail

North

Chippewa
Falls

Black River

Ski Ramp

Chairlift

Gift
Shop

Service Road

Entrance Road

Copper Peak
Mountain Bike Park

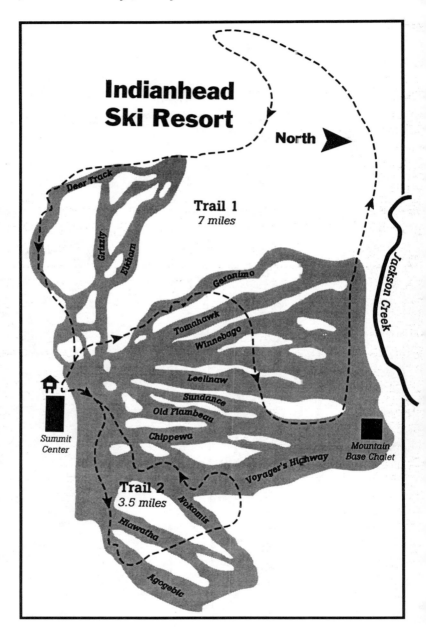

Indianhead Ski Resort

North

Deer Track

Grizzly

Elkhorn

Trail 1
7 miles

Geronimo

Tomahawk

Winnebago

Jackson Creek

Leelinaw

Sundance

Old Piambeau

Chippewa

Summit Center

Trail 2
3.5 miles

Nokomis

Hiawatha

Agogebic

Voyager's Highway

Mountain Base Chalet

Indianhead Ski Resort

County: Gogebic
Total Mileage: 12.5 miles
Terrain: Ski hills
Fees: None
Difficulty: Strenuous

Indianhead, perhaps the Upper Peninsula's best known golf and ski resort, added mountain biking in 1995 after an avid off-road cyclist in its maintenance department laid out a course on the downhill runs. There are no trail fees at Indianhead nor do you have to be an overnight guest at the lodge to ride here.

The 12.5-mile system begins from the Summit Center, the day-use lodge for skiers in the winter, and is divided among three separate loops. The newest loop is a 2-mile single track that departs east and follows a series of switchbacks to descend Indianhead Mountain into an area that was recently logged out.

The most popular rides, and the routes described here, are the original two loops that depart north from the Summit Center and descend the mountain along the wide, grassy downhill ski runs. Trail 1 is more difficult than Trail 2, but both are challenging rides due to the rapid downhill runs and the heart-pounding climbs back to the top.

225

A wide range of accommodations and other facilities are offered at Indianhead from spring through fall. If you don't have a bike, Trek and Trail in Ironwood ☎ (906-932-5858) rents mountain bikes and will arrange to have them dropped-off at the resort.

Getting There: From Wakefield head west on US-2 to Indianhead Mountain Road where the ski resort is well posted. Head north on Indianhead Mountain Road to the Summit Center at the end.

Information: Contact Indianhead Resort, 500 Indianhead RD., Wakefield, MI 49968; ☎ (906) 229-5181 or ☎ (800) 346-3426.

Trail 1
Distance: 7 miles
Trail: Ski hills, single track and forest road
Direction: Counter clockwise

The trailhead is on west side of the Summit Center and from there mountain bike symbols lead you onto either Trail 1 or Trail 2. Trail 1 heads west underneath the triple chair lift and through some small patches of woods to emerge near the top of the Geronimo Run, a black diamond slope in the winter for skiers.

It's a rapid descent on the upper half of this slope. You need to be careful as this is a steep downhill stretch with water bars. Eventually bike symbols lead you off the slope and through some short segments of single track in the woods as you cross four ski slopes. You emerge in a bowl formed by Sundance and Old Flambeau runs where you finish the downhill run to the bottom of the mountain.

Near the Mountain Base Chalet the trail swings west, skirts the bottom of the slopes, passes the T-bar lift at the end of Geronimo Run, and within a half mile swings into the woods along a forest road. Follow the road through the woods for the next 2 miles until breaking out at the double chair lift at the bottom of Deer Track Run.

The final leg of the ride is a mile-long climb up this slope to Summit Center. Although rated *Easiest* for skiers, Deer Track is still a brutal climb back up to the top of the mountain.

Trail 2

Distance: 3.5 miles
Trail: Ski hills and single track
Direction: Counter clockwise

Although still a challenging ride, Trail 2 is not as long nor does it possess the wild downhill run of Trail 1. From the Summit Center trailhead you swing east and begin by riding along the tops of the ski runs on the east side of the mountain.

The trail then heads down Agogebic Run partially before swinging west to enter the woods on a single track. You break out at Hiawatha Run, re-enter the woods, break out at Nokomis and re-enter the woods one more time. You emerge on Voyager's Highway near a sundeck. The climb back to Summit Center is along this slope rated *Easiest* for skiers.

Upper Peninsula
Road Routes

A biker pauses to admire views of Lake Michigan and the Mackinac Bridge along the St. Ignace road route.

Wander Around The Straits

County: Mackinac
Starting Point: Ferry parking lot, St. Ignace
Distance: 18 miles
Terrain: Flat to rolling, few steep hills
Highlights: St. Ignace, Lake Michigan, Mackinac Bridge view
Suggested riders: Beginner to intermediate

More than 4 million vehicles cross the Mackinac Bridge annually and most of them continue either north on I-75 or west along US-2. On this road route we invite you to stay and circle St. Ignace for an enjoyable ride along the lightly traveled Boulevard Drive. High point of the 18-mile trip are the panoramic views of the "Mighty Mac," one of the largest suspension bridges in the country.

St. Ignace, located on the north side of the bridge, serves as a hub for tourists because of its strategic location near Mackinac Island. Founded by Father Marquette in 1671, St. Ignace is the oldest city in Michigan and features a rich history that begins with the Native Americans and extends through the 17th century fur trade. As a vacation base, you can make excursions to Mackinac Island or other Upper Peninsula attractions such as Tahquamenon Falls.

Or stay in the area and enjoy a morning of cycling. Start your bicycle route at the Gandy Dancer, a refurbished depot where you can fuel up on pancakes or other breakfast food. The route heads north out of St. Ignace, goes west on backroads past wildflowers, woods, snowmobile trails and open country before following Lake Michigan back to St. Ignace. Although the majority of the route is paved, hybrid or mountain bikes are recommended because a portion of the ride is on a gravel road.

Stage one (6.9 miles) From the Star Line parking lot in downtown St. Ignace, near the Gandy Dancer Restaurant, turn right on State Street, which heads north out of town. The brick sidewalks along this road will be bustling during the summer before you leave St. Ignace. You'll pass a Pizza Hut, the Arnold Line ferry docks, several motels and an IGA store. Turn left on Murray Road at **Mile 1.2** and then a quick right on Lemottee at **Mile 1.4**. This road, which becomes Cheeseman Road, goes under the highway and then through a forested terrain of pines, hardwoods, rocky outcroppings and wildflowers.

The road features gravel shoulders and can be bumpy in places. After a couple of sharp curves, it includes some fairly steep uphills. Along this journey there are plenty of dirt roads and snowmobile trails for detours with a mountain bike. After a sharp downhill you reach US-2 just before **Mile 7**. Be careful crossing this busy artery to the western half of the Upper Peninsula.

Stage two (5.6 miles) On the other side of US-2 Cheeseman Road ends. Turn left (south) on Gros Cap Road and follow this lightly traveled road as it twists and turns along the forested Lake Michigan shoreline and past a restored church. Eventually the road ends back at US-2, which you follow for a

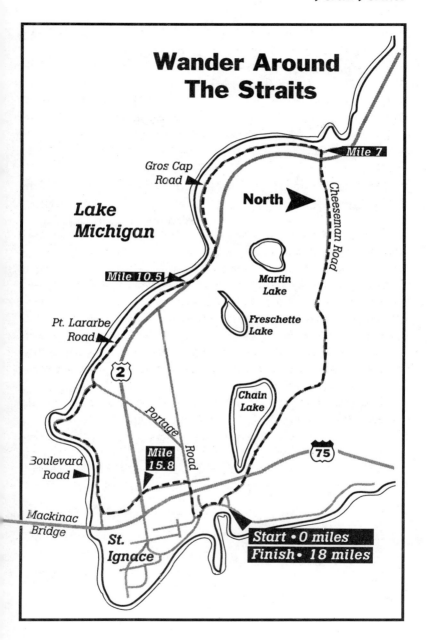

Wander Around The Straits

North ▶

Gros Cap Road ▶

Mile 7

Lake Michigan

Cheeseman Road

Mile 10.5 ▶

Martin Lake

Freschette Lake

Pt. Lararbe Road ▶

(2)

Portage Road

Chain Lake

Mile 15.8

(75)

Boulevard Road ▶

Mackinac Bridge

St. Ignace

Start • 0 miles
Finish • 18 miles

short spell to the right (east). Again this highway can be very busy though it does feature a wide paved shoulder.

You pass a tourist stop called Deer Ranch, Silver Sands Resort and a ranger station for the Hiawatha National Forest before you turn right on Point Lararbe Road at *Mile 10.5*. This forested road features far less traffic than US-2 and allows you to enjoy glimpses of the Mackinac Bridge. Turn right on Boulevard Drive at *Mile 12.5*.

Stage three (5.4 miles) Boulevard Road is the high-light of this tour as it hugs the shoreline for more great views of the Mighty Mac along with picturesque islands in Lake Michigan. At *Mile 12.9* the road turns to hard-packed gravel for almost 2 miles and then back to pavement. Boulevard Road goes uphill to the left at *Mile 15.4* and you need to make a right onto US-2 at *Mile 15.8*. At a Shell Station turn left on an old service road that parallels I-75.

Follow this road north as it heads uphill and makes a right on Spring Street, followed by another right on Second Street, and a right on Portage Street at *Mile 16.8*. At a fork Portage Street veers to the left and at *Mile 17.3* turn right onto State Street to return to the starting point. Or take a break here at the Just Right Bakery on the corner. How convenient! This ride ends back at the Star Line parking lot at *Mile 18*. Time to buy your UP souvenirs, sample a pasty or hop a ferry to Mackinac Island.

Bicycle Sales, Service
Balsam Sports, 20 N. State St., St. Ignace; ☎ (906) 643-6395.

Travel Information
St. Ignace Area Chamber of Commerce, St. Ignace Tourist Association; ☎ (800) 338-6660, ☎ (906) 643-8717.

Island Tour To DeTour

Counties: Mackinac, Chippewa
Starting Point: Cedarville
Distance: 65 Miles
Terrain: Primarily flat
Highlights: Lake Huron islands, DeTour, freighters on St. Mary's River
Suggested riders: Intermediate

This 65-mile loop from Cedarville to DeTour could also be called the "Island Tour." You don't actually cycle on any islands along this ride but pass more than 50 of them while following M-134 including Drummond Island. There are also lots of sand dunes and shoreline views along this nicely paved state highway, which accounts for a third of the route.

In DeTour, the southern entrance to the St. Mary's River, take an extended break and participate in a local pastime; freighter watching. Often a string of Great Lakes and foreign freighters navigate the river during the shipping season on their way to either Lake Superior or Lake Huron. A good place to watch the freighters is by the town's public marina.

Cyclists who want to camp have several campgrounds to choose from, including the rustic DeTour State Forest Campground along M-134 and Boundary Waters and Spring Bay, commercial campgrounds in DeTour.

Stage one (17.2 miles) Begin your ride by the water at the Cedarville Mooring & Launching Facility. This marina is next to the Cedarville Bar and across the street from Popp's Deli & Catering - a spot afterwards for pizza, ice cream and subs. Cycle left out of the parking lot and turn right on Meridian Street past the impressive boats in Cedarville's large marina. Turn right (east) on M-134, a road with wide paved shoulders. You immediately cycle through a commercial strip that includes an outdoor store, several motels and a hardware store and finally pass a highway sign announcing it's only 23 miles to DeTour.

Loon Point Campground is reached at **Mile 1.7** and is followed by a downhill and a long, gradual uphill to **Mile 2**. You're treated to an occasional view of Lake Huron through the trees and then, after crossing Prentiss Creek at **Mile 7**, your first scattering of islands.

Chippewa County is entered at **Mile 13.2** and after crossing Trout Creek you reach a small roadside park just past **Mile 17**. This is a good place to catch your breath before cycling the remaining 7 miles to DeTour.

Stage two (7.7 miles) The next stretch is stunning from early to mid-October, when the fall colors are peaking along the lakeshore here. There are plenty of hardwoods on both sides of the road before you reach the DeTour State Forest Campground at **Mile 18.4**. The campground features 21 rustic sites, most of them with a view of Lake Huron along with a swimming beach and a picnic area.

Stretches of open water are viewed before you enter the village of DeTour near **Mile 23**. A pleasant picnic area with tables and benches is located just beyond the DeTour Passage Launch Ramp at **Mile 23.7** and is followed by the DeTour Family Campground and a memorial garden. You reach the business district of DeTour at **Mile 24.5**. Time for a meal at a local restaurant, a picnic by the water or some freighter watching in

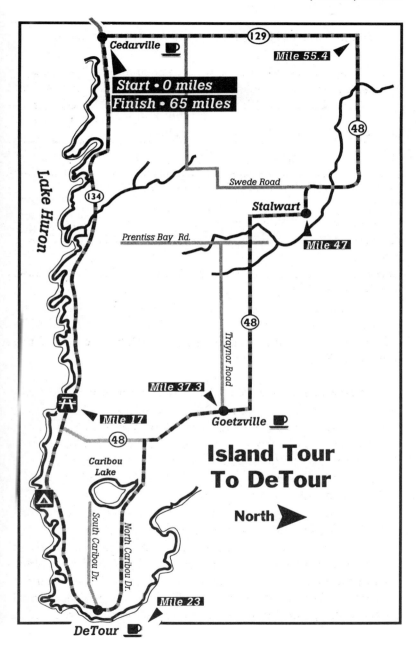

Cedarville

129 Mile 55.4

Start • 0 miles
Finish • 65 miles

48

134 Swede Road

Stalwart

Prentiss Bay Rd.

Mile 47

48

Traynor Road

Mile 37.3

Mile 17 Goetzville

48 **Island Tour To DeTour**

Caribou Lake

North

South Caribou Dr.

North Caribou Dr.

Lake Huron

Mile 23

DeTour

DeTour.

Stage three (22.3 miles) Head west out of town on Ontario Street, past the Harbor House Bakery, the DeTour Village Motel and Dockside Cafe. Ontario Street becomes Democrat Road when it climbs a hill and makes a couple of sharp curves leading you past birch and other hardwoods that are exceptionally colorful in the fall.

Democrat Road turns into North Caribou Drive, meanders over some hills and then skirts Caribou Lake. At **Mile 30.5** you pass a public access site to the lake and a half mile later turn right (north) on M-48, which has a mixture of asphalt and gravel shoulders. After a couple of curves M-48 becomes a flat straightaway into the town of Goetzville, reached at **Mile 37.3**. This burg consists of a few small businesses, cottages and a couple of gas stations.

At **Mile 42**, M-48 swings west into more flat, open country that makes for easy riding for the next few miles past picturesque farms. Eventually M-48 swings north and reaches the small burg of Stalwart at **Mile 47**.

Stage four (17.8 miles) At Stalwart, M-48 curves west briefly, north again at Mile 48 and then west once more. After crossing the East Branch of the Munuscong River at **Mile 53.8** you reach a major intersection with M-129 at **Mile 55.4**. Turn left (south) to return to Cedarville. A mixture of paved and gravel shoulders, M-129 heads due south reaching the Cedarville marina where you started at **Mile 65**.

Travel information
DeTour Chamber of Commerce; ☎ (906) 297-5987.
Drummond Island Chamber of Commerce; ☎ (906) 493-5245; ☎ (800) 737-8666.

Lakes of the Northwoods

Counties: Schoolcraft, Luce and Mackinac
Starting Point: Germfask
Distance: 31 miles
Terrain: Flat with some hills
Highlights: Seney Wildlife Area, Curtis, Manistique Lake
Suggested Riders: Intermediate

The stretch of road on M-77 near Seney National Wildlife Refuge is remembered by most travelers as a long, boring stretch of road. Cyclists will be pleasantly surprised, however, by this road route as it is yet another example of why you need to slow down - via two wheels - to fully enjoy a region.

The route winds its way through Curtis, a unique waterfront village of cabins, sporting goods stores and shops. Curtis is in the heart of what is often described as the largest collection of inland lakes in Michigan, with several small towns situated around six lakes. This makes the area an excellent one for a variety of recreation. While you cycle, others can fish, canoe the Manistique River or enjoy the unusual Wildlife Auto Tour at Seney National Wildlife Refuge.

Stage one (11.2 miles) The route around Manistique Lakes begins in the small town of Germfask on M-77. A good place to park is the Germfask Trading Post and an excellent place for a bite to eat before or after the r de is the Eagle's Nest Restaurant just up the road.

Head south on M-77 briefly and then make a left on County Road H-44 that immediately crosses the Manistique River. The road curves up and around Manistique Lake and features gravel shoulders and light traffic. Before you reach Luce County at **Mile 4.4** you cross the Manistique River again and cruise through a lush mix of pines, hardwoods and birch trees.

There's a long gradual uphill beginning at **Mile 7.3** that tops off at a Mobil station if you're suddenly in need of a snack. CR H-44 passes several resorts and cottages and then a county park and campground on the left at **Mile 11.2**.

Stage two (7.1 miles) Continue on CR H-44 and you'll enjoy a long downhill to Helmer and a market. Turn right (south) on CR H-33 toward Curtis. *Be aware; this road features gravel shoulders and can be busy at times.* CR H-33 skirts Manistique Lake and then enters Mackinac County at **Mile 14.3**. At this point the road narrows and becomes a bit bumpier. Before you reach Curtis at **Mile 17.6** you will pass the historic Chamberlin's Ole Forest Inn (☎ 906-586-6000). Originally a railroad hotel that was built in the late 1800s in Curtis, the inn was moved to its present location on a bluff above the lake in 1924 by sliding it across the ice. Today it features 10 rooms, an excellent restaurant and a veranda where you can enjoy the view and breeze off Manistique Lake.

Turn right on CR H-42 into the business district of Curtis with more cottages, boat rentals, gift shops and motels. In town there's plenty of places for a food break with an IGA store, pizza and sub shop and ice cream parlor on your left at **Mile 18.3**.

Stage three (12.3 miles) South Manistique Lake is visible on the left as you make your way up a hill and out of Curtis. At **Mile 19**, CR H-42 makes a right turn (north) and

climbs for a half mile to a left-hand curve at **Mile 19.7**. This is followed by another long, gradual uphill. The Log Cabin Resort and Campground (☎ 906-586-9732) and Trails Inn Resort (☎ 906-586-3515) are passed just before **Mile 22**. There are also some scenic views of Manistique Lake here before a bumpy CR H-42 curves to the right and begins climbing.

The road stays bumpy as you make your way back to M-77, enjoying a long downhill and then enduring an uphill stretch along the way. M-77 is reached at **Mile 28.3**. There's a nice roadside park with vault toilets on the right just before you cross the Manistique River at **Mile 29.3**. A sign for the Northern Hardwoods Cross Country Ski Area is passed at **Mile 30**, followed by the Big Cedar Campground and Canoe Rental (☎ 906-586-6684). You reach your starting point, the Germfask Trading Post at **Mile 30.6**.

Optional mileage: For an interesting side trip, continue north on M-77 for 3.2 miles to the Seney National Wildlife Area. The Visitor Center features a variety of displays, audiovisual room and wildlife observation area overlooking a pond and wetlands. The Seney National Wildlife Refuge was established in 1935 for the protection and production of migratory birds and other wildlife. The refuge features 95,455 acres of marsh, ponds field and forest and is known for its diversity of wildlife species. The best way to view the interior is with a mountain bike on the network of graveled dikes (see page 59).

Bicycle Rental
Northland Outfitters, Germfask; ☎ (906) 586-9801.

Travel Information
Curtis Area Chamber of Commerce; ☎ (800) 652-8784 or ☎ (906) 586-3700.

Manistique Lakes Area Tourist Assn.; ☎ (800) 860-3820.

Back To Paradise

County: Chippewa
Starting point: Paradise
Distance: 88 miles
Terrain: Mostly flat
Highlights: Whitefish Bay, Lake Superior shoreline
Suggested Riders: Intermediate

This is paradise??? Paradise, the town, has a population of 500 and is mostly a collection of small motels, cafes, gas stations and cheesey gift shops.

But the surrounding area is stunning in terms of the spectacular scenery found in this corner of the Upper Peninsula. Often called the "Gateway to Tahquamenon," Paradise is within 12 miles of the famous Tahquamenon Falls while to the north is Whitefish Point, home of the Great Lakes Shipwreck Museum. To the south, roads skirt the shores of Whitefish Bay almost all the way to Sault Ste. Marie, making Paradise an ideal starting point for a long but easy road route with plenty of opportunities to stop and soak up the scenery.

The high point of this 74-mile ride is the Whitefish Bay Scenic Byway, one of only two in Michigan. Also called Lewis Memorial Highway, more aptly described as Lakeshore Drive, the byway makes up a 20-mile stretch of the ride and allows you to follow the Lake Superior shoreline, enjoying its windswept dunes and scenic vistas.

This route can also be extended to cover more than 100 miles by beginning and ending at Upper Tahquamenon Falls. Or the ride can be part of a weekend of camping by securing one of the 300 sites within four campgrounds at Tahquamenon Falls State Park. If you wish to pack along the gear and break the route into two days of riding, there is Bay View National Forest Campground. Located on the route, this 24-site campground is a rustic facility (vault toilets, hand-pumped water) in a very scenic setting on the shores of Whitefish Bay.

Stage one (11.4 miles) From the business area of Paradise cycle south on M-123, passing many restaurants for now or later as well as a small IGA grocery store. Leaving town M-123 is a flat road with paved shoulders. You'll enjoy glimpses of Whitefish Bay before crossing a bridge with narrow shoulders over the Tahquamenon River at **Mile 5.4** and passing the entrance to the campground of the Rivermouth Unit of Tahquamenon Falls State Park.

A level straightaway follows and leads you into the Hiawatha National Forest at **Mile 10.8**. At **Mile 11.4** you reach Lewis Memorial Highway (Lakeshore Drive), the west end of the Whitefish Bay National Scenic Byway.

Stage two (19.9 miles) Lakeshore Drive curves to the left and skirts the beautiful Lake Superior shoreline. You ride through some dips before passing a trailhead of the North Country Trail at **Mile 14.8**. Roxbury Creek is crossed at **Mile 16.2,** where more views of the shoreline can be enjoyed through a mix of hardwoods and pines. Naomikong Creek is crossed at **Mile 18.3** and is followed by a long, gradual uphill that crests in three-quarters of a mile at another sign for the North Country Trail. The road twists and curves before you reach Halfaday Creek at **Mile 22.6**. On this stretch of Lakeshore Drive there are many spots to enjoy the breezes and scenery of Lake Superior.

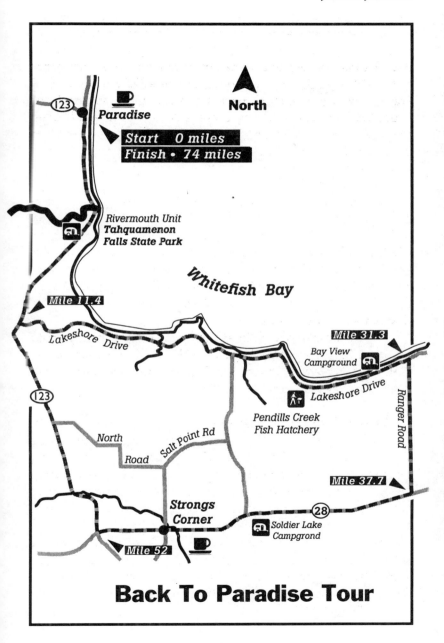

North

Paradise

Start   0 miles
Finish • 74 miles

Rivermouth Unit
Tahquamenon
Falls State Park

Whitefish Bay

Mile 11.4

Lakeshore Drive

Mile 31.3

Bay View
Campground

Lakeshore Drive

Pendills Creek
Fish Hatchery

Ranger Road

North

Road

Salt Point Rd

Mile 37.7

Strongs
Corner

Soldier Lake
Campgrond

Mile 52

Back To Paradise Tour

After leveling out, Lakeshore Drive passes Pendills Creek National Fish Hatchery at **Mile 27**. Built in 1952, the hatchery today features 16 raceways where more than two million lake trout fingerlings are produced annually for stocking in the Great Lakes. The hatchery is open Monday through Friday from 8 a.m. to 4:30 p.m. and visitors are welcome to wander around the raceways to see the fish. Display boards covering the life cycle of lake trout, restrooms and drinking water make this a nice place for an extended break.

At **Mile 29.3** is Bay View Campground and another mile east is Big Pine Picnic Area. Both national forest facilities are nestled among pines and along one of the most beautiful beaches in the Upper Peninsula. Okay, so maybe you can't swim except for those three days in August when the temperature breaks 90 degrees up here. But you can walk the beach in either direction and reflect on the lake they call "Gitche Gumme."

At **Mile 31.3** turn right at the stop sign on Ranger Road by the abandoned train car of the Soo Line.

Stage three (20.8 miles) Ranger Road features wide, gravel shoulders and climbs a bit before leveling out on its way to M-28. Turn right on M-28 at **Mile 37.7**. This can be a busy highway on holidays and weekends and is bumpy in spots, but it has wide shoulders of pavement and gravel. Cycle past Soldier Lake National Forest Campground, another possible spot for a break, and cross over the East Branch of the Tahquamenon River at **Mile 48.7**. You climb to the hamlet of Strongs Corner where there is Lamplighter Restaurant and Motel and a small convenience store. Turn right on M-123 at **Mile 52**, following the signs to Tahquamenon Falls State Park.

Stage four (22 miles) Head north on M-123 through the village of Eckerman before crossing the East Branch of the Tahquamenon River again at **Mile 54.5**. This road is primarily flat so you can pick up speed. You return to the intersection with Lakeshore Drive at **Mile 63** and then retrace the 11 miles

A possible starting point for this ride is at the Upper Tahquamenon Falls, one of the largest cascades east of the Mississippi River.

of M-123 back to Paradise, reaching the town at **Mile 74**.

Time to try what the locals recommend - a cinnamon roll at the Paradise Restaurant, an artery-clogging Yukon Burger (ground beef, ham, bacon and cheese) at the Yukon Inn or a whitefish dinner at the Little Falls Inn.

Option for Century Ride (100 miles): By beginning and ending your ride on M-123 at Upper Tahquamenon Falls you can turn this route into a century ride. It is 14 miles from the upper falls to Paradise which would add 28 miles for a total of 102 miles. Keep in mind M-123 can be busy during any summer weekend.

Travel information

Tahquamenon Falls State Park; ☎ (906) 492-3415.
Brimley State Park; ☎ (906) 248-3422.
Paradise Area Chamber of Commerce; ☎ (906) 492-3219.
Paradise Area Tourism Council; ☎ (906) 492-3927.

Wagner Falls, the centerpiece of Michigan's smallest state park, makes for a scenic stop along the Munising tour.

Meandering Around Munising

County: Alger
Starting Point: Scott Falls Roadside Park
Distance: 32.9 miles
Terrain: Rolling hills
Highlights: Waterfalls, Lake Superior, Au Train
Suggested Riders: Intermediate

The first time I passed through Munising I was overwhelmed by its beauty. From the swampy interior of Schoolcraft County, I followed M-28 into Alger County and suddenly arrived at this comfortable town nestled around the shore of Grand Harbor. It was a clear day but the mist was rising off the bay to give Grand Island the illusion of floating on the water and reminded me, in some ways, of Hawaii.

Of course, Hawaii doesn't average 250 inches of snow each winter. But when the weather warms in the spring and the snow finally melts away in May, the Munising area can provide cyclists with a pleasant journey through some of the finest country in the U.P. With Pictured Rocks National Lakeshore nearby, you can easily round out a long weekend with a boat tour to the famed colored cliffs or an afternoon hike into Cascade Falls.

Munising boasts a wide range of motels and even a city-operated campground on the shores of Lake Superior.

This 33-mile route begins near Au Train and winds its way through a wooded resort area, past waterfalls and into Munising for ice cream or a meal. You will also cycle past a larger-than-life Santa at the end of St. Nicholas Lane in touristy Christmas. But don't despair. You're in the heart of Michigan's waterfall country and the tranquility and beauty of these cascades will restore your faith in the natural charm of Munising.

Stage one: (11.7 miles) Begin near Au Train at Scott Falls Roadside Park on M-28, where there's a beach, bathroom and picnic tables. Turn right on M-28, a state highway with a lot of traffic during the summer but also wide shoulders. You're immediately rewarded with a panoramic view of Lake Superior before turning left (south) on Au Train Forest Lake Road just beyond **Mile 1** and reach Au Train. In this tiny hamlet there are two gas stations, a deli with pasties, pizzas and subs and the Au Train Bike Shop for bike rentals.

At **Mile 1.7** cross the Coucette Bridge and head out of town. There's a blend of pines and hardwoods on this road that winds around Au Train Lake and at **Mile 5.3** passes a staging area for the North Hiawatha Snowmobile Trail. The road winds and dips with a nice downhill run at **Mile 7**. M-94 is reached at **Mile 9** and the route continues left (east) on this road, which features paved shoulders. You immediately cross the Au Train River and reach Ackerman Lake at **Mile 11.7**.

Stage two (9 miles) Journey past the Rapid River Truck Trail at **Mile 12.5** and then enjoy a long straightaway that lasts for almost 2 miles. At this point M-94 swings northeast through a series of long rolling hills and past the posted trailhead and parking area of the Valley Spur Ski Trail. This Nordic ski area also offers mountain biking opportunities on a portion of its trails during the summer. *Be careful along this stretch of M-94;*

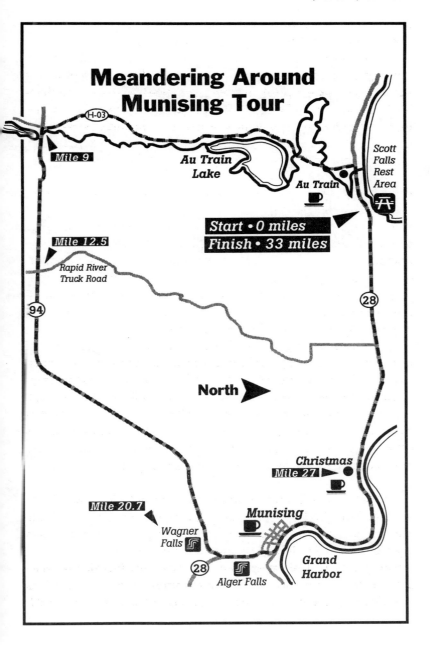

Meandering Around Munising Tour

H-03

Mile 9

Au Train Lake

Scott Falls Rest Area

Au Train

Start • 0 miles
Finish • 33 miles

Mile 12.5

Rapid River Truck Road

94

28

North

Christmas
Mile 27

Mile 20.7

Munising

Wagner Falls

28

Alger Falls

Grand Harbor

the traffic is usually light but can be very fast.

At **Mile 20.7** you reach the Wagner Fals Scenic Site. At only 22 acres, this is "Michigan's smallest state park" but not one to be passed up. Park the bikes and hike the short path and boardwalk to the falls, an aesthetic mix of woods, wildflowers and water cascading over rock ledges and fallen trees. If you packed along a lunch, this is an excellent place to enjoy it as an observation deck with benches is situated at the end of the boardwalk.

Stage three (12.2 miles) Turn left (north) onto M-28 at **Mile 21.8**. Alger Falls, visible from the road on your right, conveniently tucked on a hillside. Within a mile, you enter the heart of Munising and ample choices for food Hardees, Dairy Queen or the Dogpatch Restaurant, a sit-down place with a casual ambiance. You'll work hard climbing uphill as you head out of Munising, topping off at the posted entrance of a scenic viewpoint. Those with energy to spare might want to follow the entrance drive to this roadside park. It's a steep climb of a half mile but the view of Grand Island and the Pictured Rocks at the top is stunning. *Be careful not to gain too much speed on the way back to M-28.*

At **Mile 27**, you reach a town with a jolly theme - Christmas. There's a large statue of Santa to confirm your arrival but also a party store for cold drinks and Bay Furnace Campground and Picnic Area, a great place to dip your toes into Lake Superior. Another long uphill climb must be endured before you reach Scott Falls Roadside Park at **Mile 33**.

Travel Information

Alger County Chamber of Commerce, Munising; ☎ (906) 387-2138

Hiawatha National Forest Center, Munising; ☎ (906) 387-3700

Peninsula Point

County: Delta
Starting Point: Rapid River
Distance: 50 miles
Terrain: Mostly flat
Highlights: Lighthouse and Little Bay de Noc
Suggested Riders: Intermediate

Cyclists looking for a route into a remote corner of the Upper Peninsula should seriously consider this Peninsula Point tour. This stretch of land between the bays of Little and Big Bay de Noc in Delta County is an isolated area with no towns other than tiny Stonington and little development of any kind. The journey to reach the lighthouse at the tip of the peninsula makes you wonder how, or maybe why, people manage to live on this peninsula during those long U.P. winters.

On the other hand, during the summer the peninsula offers cyclists an area to totally escape and enjoy remote woods, wildflowers along the road and the deep blue waters of Lake Michigan. Delta County, with its Little and Big Bay de Noc, has more freshwater shoreline than any county in the state.

Pack plenty of snacks for this ride as there are few places to buy food. There are a few restaurants in Rapid River, your starting and ending point, but none after you begin the tour. Part of this route is on gravel and dirt roads so it's best ridden on either a hybrid or mountain bike. Finally, plan lunch or at least an extended break at Peninsula Point Lighthouse. It's an incredibly beautiful spot to linger for an hour or more.

Stage one (15 miles) In Rapid River there are brown signs pointing to the Masonville Township Recreation Area, a good place to start your ride. The park includes picnic tables, rest rooms and pavilions. Cycle out of the recreation area to US-2 and turn right near an IGA grocery store and a Marathon station. US-2, the main street in town, can be busy though there are shoulders on both sides of the road. You'll pass an antique shop and cross Rapid River before reaching the Hiawatha National Forest Ranger Station (☎ 906-474-6442), a great place for outdoor recreation information on the area. US-2 then crosses over Whitefish River. At **Mile 3**, turn right at the *Stonington* sign on County Road 513.

This lightly traveled road has gravel shoulders. You pass yet another Marathon station and just after **Mile 4** reach a nice stand of pine trees. The road can be bumpy in places as it climbs a couple of hills and then passes the Vagabond Resort Campground (☎ 906-474-6122). At **Mile 7.6** is a nice flat section where you can pick up the speed. Within a mile you reach Little Bay de Noc Recreation Area, a Hiawatha National Forest facility that features 36 campsites, a sandy swimming beach, picnic area and nature trails (see page 135).

There's another nice straight portion of CR-513 following the campground that extends for more than a mile. At **Mile 13.2** you pass a one-room log cabin in a pleasant manicured field and then the road narrows. A gas station and convenience store (junk food!) is reached before the road curves to the left and reaches Stonington Village Hall at **Mile 15**. Along the way there are many views of Little Bay de Noc, tipping you off that you're getting closer to the tip of the peninsula.

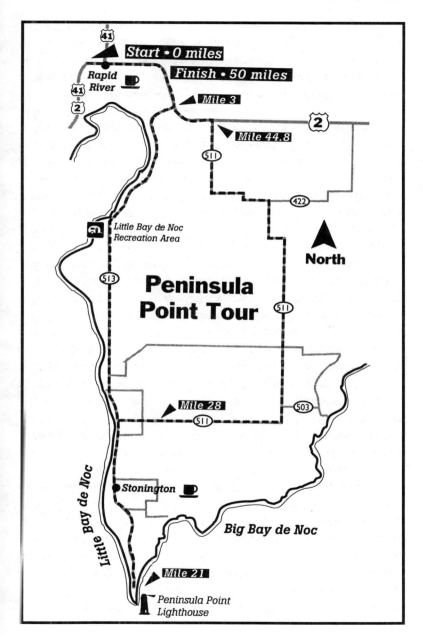

Start • 0 miles

Finish • 50 miles

Rapid River

Mile 3

Mile 44.8

Little Bay de Noc
Recreation Area

North

Peninsula
Point Tour

Mile 28

503

Stonington

Big Bay de Noc

Little Bay de Noc

Mile 21

Peninsula Point
Lighthouse

Stage two (8 miles) Stay on CR-513 to pass pictur-esque Trinity Lutheran Church at **Mile 16.3**. The road then gets considerably bumpier but there's more great views of the bay. CR-513 turns to packed gravel, returns to pavement at **Mile 18.2** and then back to gravel a mile later. It now skirts the water through an exceptional tree-lined section and nar-rows to one lane. This section is a highlight of the ride, with Black-eyed Susans and other wildflowers adding considerable color to the woods. CR-513 remains a rugged one-lane and at **Mile 21** you break out at the Peninsula Point Lighthouse. The lighthouse, built in 1865, is the focal point of this national forest picnic area at the end of the peninsula. It went out of commission in 1936 but the spot was so beautiful it became a picnic area the next year.

The lightkeeper's house burned down in 1959 and all that remains today is the 40-foot brick tower. But the circular stair-way to the top is an easy climb and the watery views of the bays are spectacular. Also located here are picnic tables, grills, vault toilets and drinking water.

Stage three (14.2 miles) Backtrack the way you came but make a right (east) on County Road 511 at **Mile 27.4**. This paved, primarily flat road has no shoulders but also little traf-fic. There's a nice straightaway near **Mile 30** followed by open country. The road curves sharply to your left at **Mile 32.6** past a scattering of houses as this stretch is not quite as remote as other earlier sections of the route. You climb a steep uphill at **Mile 34.8** followed by a long straightaway and some rolling hills starting at **Mile 35.3**.

Stage four (14 miles) CR-511 enters a series of 90-degree curves that last for almost 10 miles on the way back to US-2 and Rapid River. US-2 is reached at **Mile 44.8**; turn left. Again this road can be busy though there are paved shoulders. You reach the Rapid River at **Mile 49**. Your starting point is just a third of a mile down the road.

The highlight of the tour through Stonington Peninsula is the historic Peninsula Point Lighthouse, the halfway point of this 50-mile ride.

Bicycle Sales, Service

Bike Inn, 1815 Third Ave. N, Escanaba; ☎ (906) 789-9188.
Mr. Bike, 2329 First Ave. N, Escanaba; ☎ (906) 786-1200.

Travel information

Delta County Tourism Bureau; ☎ (800) 437-7496.

A cyclist pauses at a sandy beach along Lake Superior, a scenic spot linked to the city of Marquette by a bike path.

Marvelous Marquette Tour

County: Marquette
Starting Point: MDOT
Welcome Center
Distance: 22 miles
Terrain: Flat to rolling hills, plus a
mile-long hill
Highlights: Lake Superior, Presque Isle Park
Sugested Riders: Intermediate

The metropolitan center of the Upper Peninsula, and some would say the only true city north of the Mackinac Bridge, is Marquette. Home of 22,000 residents plus an additional 8,000 college students at Northern Michigan University, Marquette is a hilly, scenic town along the shores of Lake Superior with all the amenities of any Michigan city. But this historic iron ore town is also surrounded by a natural resource base that is second to none in any region of Michigan. Its vast forests, nearby wilderness areas, lakes and shorelines invite you to spend your days kayaking, mountain biking, cross country skiing or tossing a fly in a gurgling stream in search of wild brook trout.

One of the most impressive natural features of Marquette is Presque Isle Park, which is French for "almost an island" but is fondly referred to by many locals as simply "The Island." Situated north of the downtown area, the 328-acre park occupies a small peninsula and features a shoreline of steep cliffs that resemble the famous bluffs at Pictured Rocks near Munising.

Presque Isle is the highpoint of this 22-mile ride around Marquette. The majority of the route follows a bike path along the perimeter of the city that was completed in 1996. You begin and end the ride at the Michigan Department of Transportation Welcome Center, a classic log cabin on the shores of Lake Superior, where you can gather brochures and suggestions on a variety of other activities in the Marquette area to round out your vacation.

Stage one (6 miles) Park at the MDOT Welcome Center, south of Marquette on US-41. The center not only has racks of travel information for throughout the U.P., but also bathrooms and drinking water. A paved bike path heads north along Lake Superior but ends at Lake Street at *Mile 1.4*. Turn right on Lake Street, left on Hampton Road and right on US-41 just beyond *Mile 2*. You return to the bike path by turning right on Baraga to Lakeshore to enter Ellwood A. Matson Lower Harbor Park at *Mile 2.5*. The park, the site of many summer activities in Marquette, can be an alternative starting point for this tour. Located here is an ice cream shop, grills, restrooms, a grassy picnic area and a marina.

Back on the bike path you follow the shoreline along Marquette Harbor, swing north and pass the Marquette Maritime Museum, catching a glimpse of the bright red Marquette Lighthouse nearby. By the Lakeshore Bike Shop cross the street to continue north on the bike path to Presque Isle.

You reach the entrance of the park at *Mile 6*, where you'll be overwhelmed by the iron ore dock along the shoreline here. If you're lucky they will be loading a freighter with ore pellets, an incredible sight to see.

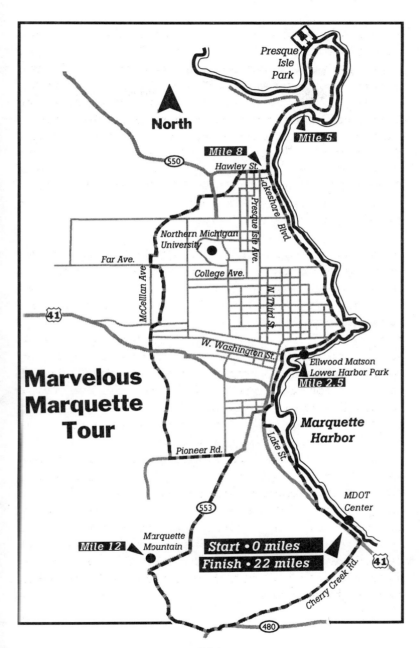

Presque
Isle
Park

North

550

Hawley St.

Mile 8

Mile 5

Lakeshore Blvd.

Presque Isle Ave.

Northern Michigan
University

Far Ave.

College Ave.

McCellan Ave.

N. Third St.

41

W. Washington St.

Ellwood Matson
Lower Harbor Park

Mile 2.5

**Marvelous
Marquette
Tour**

*Marquette
Harbor*

Pioneer Rd.

Lake St.

MDOT
Center

553

Mile 12

Marquette
Mountain

Start • 0 miles
Finish • 22 miles

41

Cherry Creek Rd.

480

Stage two (5.5 miles) Stay to your right entering the park to follow the one-way road along the water and then up and around the scenic cliffs overlooking Lake Superior. You share the road with vehicles but the speed limit is only 15 mph, and wind around several beautiful vantage points as well as climb a few mild hills. Take time to hop off the bike at the overlooks, especially at the northwest corner of the park where it's possible to see Sugarloaf, Hogsback and several other peaks north of the city. There's also an ice cream stand near the park's exit.

Backtrack on Lakeshore Road and then turn right on Hawley Street at **Mile 9** to remain on the bike path. Within a half mile you need to cross the street and then make a hard left to stay on the bike path. Cross Wright Street to skirt Northern Michigan University, where occasionally in the summer you can see and hear the marching band practice. Loop around the Upper Peninsula Medical Center on the bike path before you head south on McClellan Avenue.

Be careful as this section of McClellan can be busy, especially at the intersection with US-41. But don't be disheartened as most of McClellan features a bike path past here.

Stage three (3.5 miles) Past the US-41 intersection, McClellan Avenue has far less traffic. Cross McClellan to the east side to return to the bike path. You pass a school at **Mile 11** before crossing the street on an iron covered bridge. After the bridge, the bike path becomes a delightful ride, featuring dips, rolling hills and curves.

When McClellan Avenue ends, turn left (east) on Pioneer Road, a pleasant jaunt with paved shoulders. You'll journey by some nice houses and a trailer park before turning right (south) on CR-553, and climb some hills before reaching Marquette Mountain Ski Area at **Mile 12**. Although there's no skiing in the summer (the U.P. doesn't get that much snow!), there are outdoor concerts and picnics every week at the mountain that makes a nice respite if your timing is right.

Stage four (10 miles) Past Marquette Mountain you'll climb the largest, steepest grade on the route. Here you can whip those legs into shape and test out the gears as you sit and stand and sit and stand to make your way up this hill that is more than a mile long. Things do get easier as you approach the Crossroads, the junction of CR-553 and CR-480. Travel east on Cherry Creek Road to hook back up on US-41 and the bike path. Turn left on US-41 and head north to return to the MDOT Center, reached at **Mile 22**.

Time to savor your accomplishment with the many restaurants of Marquette. Local cyclists recommend Babycakes for muffins and coffee, located across from City Hall on Washington Street a block from The Bike Rack, a popular bike shop. Another excellent spot is Vierling Saloon & Sample Room, overlooking Marquette's Lower Harbor on Front Street and featuring its own micro-brewery. For good cafe latte and vegetarian fare there's Sweet Water Cafe on Third Street and for the best pasties in town (a Yooper delicacy) try Jean Kay's Pasty Shop on Presque Isle Street.

Bicycle Sales, Service

Bike Rack, 315 West Washington, Marquette: ☎ (906) 225-1766.

Down Wind Sports, 514 North 3rd St. Marquette ☎ (906) 226-7112.

Lakeshore Bike & Kite, 505 Lake Shore Blvd., Marquette; ☎ (906) 226-7547.

Quick Stop Bike Shop, 260 W. Magnetic, Marquette; ☎ (906) 225-1577.

Area events and festivals

July: Marquette City Band Concerts, every Thursday at 7:30 p.m., Presque Isle Bandshell; International Food Fest, Ellwood Matson Lower Harbor Park; Art on the Rocks, Presque Isle

Park.

August: Marquette City Band Concerts, every Thursday at 7:30 p.m., Presque Isle Bandshell; Chocolay Summerfest, Harvey; Marquette County Fair; FinnFest USA, Marquette.

September: Autumn Colorama, Marquette County; Antique Show & Sale, Marquette.

Travel Information

Marquette Country Convention & Visitors Bureau, ☎ (800) 544-4321, (906) 228-7749.

Marquette Area Chamber of Commerce, ☎ (906) 226-6591.

Ishpeming-Negaunee Chamber of Commerce, ☎ (906) 486-4841.

Brockway Mountain

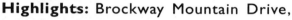

County: Keweenaw
Starting Point: Fort
Wilkins State Park
Distance: 32 miles
Terrain: Steep hills
Highlights: Brockway Mountain Drive,
Lake Superior, lighthouses
Suggested Riders: Advanced

This may be one of the most challenging and the most spectacular rides in Michigan. The scenery in the northern tip of the Keweenaw Peninsula is unsurpassed with its many views of Lake Superior and the red rocky shoreline unique to the area. But a good portion of this route is Brockway Mountain Drive, which rises more than 700 feet above Lake Superior, making it both a heart-pounding ride and possibly the most scenic road in the Midwest for cyclists to marvel at the views.

This 32-mile route begins and ends in Copper Harbor at the tip of the peninsula. This charming town features a wide range of accommodations, both campgrounds and motels, as well as restaurants, gift shops and even a public sauna to soothe those sore muscles after enduring Brockway Mountain Drive.

An ideal place to start your ride is Fort Wilkins State Park, a wooden stockade built in 1844 by the U.S. Army. The fort sits on a strip of land between Lake Superior and Lake Fanny Hooe, the perfect place to enjoy the region's natural beauty. As well as the preserved fort, which features 12 of its original structures, the park also includes two miles of shoreline on Lake Fanny Hooe, a modern campground and a beautiful picnic area.

Fees: There is an vehicle entry fee, either a daily permit or an annual state park pass, if you begin and end your ride at Fort Wilkins State Park. The permit will also allow you to view the fort and the displays in many of the buildngs. To reserve a campsite at the park call ☎ (800) 44-PARKS.

Stage one (5.8 miles) From the visitor parking lot of Fort Wilkins State Park turn left onto US-41. You're immediately rewarded with views of the water and Copper Harbor Lighthouse far to the north and at **Mile 0.4** there's a lighthouse overlook. *Be careful on this road as the traffic entering the park can be heavy at times.* You'll reach the heart of Copper Harbor at **Mile 1.2**, where there is a general store, gas station, art gallery, restaurants and the Minnetonika Resort (☎ 906-289-4449), which has Finnish sauna baths that are open to the public. When US-41 curves to the south, continue straight on M-26, passing the Old Country Store and Gratiot Street Cafe and then the Copper Harbor Marina at **Mile 2**.

Get your leg muscles ready, here we go! Just past the marina, head left onto Brockway Mountain Drive, where you immediately begin climbing. The climb levels out twice in the first mile, the second time at a scenic lookout, where you can gaze down on the town of Copper Harbor and Lake Fanny Hooe. This is a great place to take a well-deserved break.

Continuing up, you'll be able to test those granny gears as Brockway Mountain Drive continues to rise. Just past **Mile 3** is the edge of some steep cliffs. Whoa! At this height above Lake Superior it feels like you're at the edge of the earth.

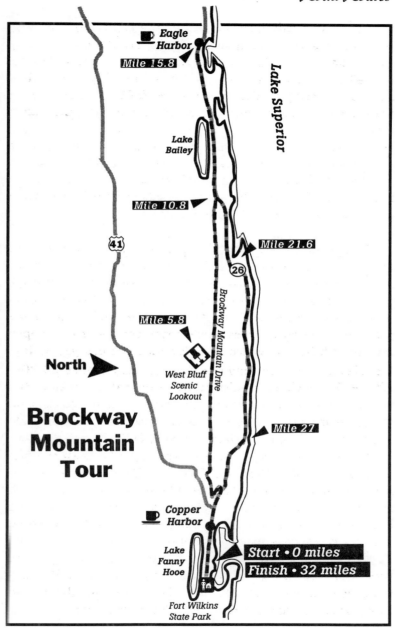

Eagle Harbor
Mile 15.8

Lake Superior

Lake Bailey

Mile 10.8

Mile 21.6

41

26

Mile 5.8

Brockway Mountain Drive

North

West Bluff Scenic Lookout

Mile 27

Brockway Mountain Tour

Copper Harbor

Lake Fanny Hooe

Start • 0 miles

Finish • 32 miles

Fort Wilkins State Park

Brockway Mountain Drive has no shoulders but most of the summer is lightly traveled. Get some momentum on a downhill at *Mile 3.6* to climb the next hill. The road is a bit bumpy as you descend another hill at *Mile 4* and a warning sign pops up: *Steep Hill*. You climb the twisting road and then enjoy a downhill run at *Mile 5* only to be confronted with another Steep Hill sign. Here Brockway Mountain Drive narrows and becomes bumpy in spots with no guardrails along the cliffs to the south. You must endure yet another steep climb before finally reaching the West Bluff Scenic Lookout at *Mile 5.8*.

Definitely stop here and soak up the view on both sides of the road. At 735 feet above Lake Superior and 1,337 feet above sea level, this is a stunning place to stretch those legs.

Stage two (10.8 miles) Continue on Brockway Mountain Drive as it heads downhill. At *Mile 6.4* you resume climbing along a twisting road with bumpy shoulders that is followed by more up and down, up and down, and, well, you get the picture. Brockway Mountain Drive doesn't level out until it almost ends at *Mile 10.8*. Turn left on M-26 (also called Lakeshore Drive) and head west to skirt the north shore of Lake Bailey. In less than 2 miles after passing the lake you will come into view of Eagle Harbor and then enter the town of the same name.

Follow this beautiful bay through town and ride to the Eagle Harbor Light Station, a bright red lighthouse on the west side, reached at *Mile 15.8*. Built in 1851, 21 lightkeepers kept a vigil watch at this station until the U.S. Coast Guard automated it in 1980. Two years later the lightkeeper's residence was turned into a delightful museum. Outside there are a few picnic tables and a beach nearby, making this the ideal spot to take a mid-ride break.

Eagle Harbor is one of the most picturesque towns in Michigan. Named after the Eagle Harbor Mining Company that began a mining operation nearby in 1845, Eagle Harbor is a sleepy little hamlet spread along the protective shore of its namesake harbor. There are restaurants, ice cream parlors and plenty of beach for an extended break.

Stage three (15.4 miles) Begin your return to Copper Harbor by heading east on M-26 and backtracking the last 5 miles. At **Mile 20.8**, you arrive at the intersection with Brockway Mountain Drive but will stay on M-26. This road, with paved shoulders, has great views of the water and rock outcroppings along Lake Superior. A great place to explore the red rocky shoreline is a roadside park reached at **Mile 21.6**.

You pass another park with picnic tables on the right at **Mile 27** before reaching the Copper Harbor Marina at **Mile 30**. Stay on US-41 to return to Fort Wilkins State Park at **Mile 32**. Tired and sore? Head to Minnetonka Resort and rent a sauna for an hour.

Bicycle Sales, Service

Dick's Favorite Sports, 1700 W. Memorial Dr., Houghton; ☎ (906) 482-0412.

Down Wind Sports, 520 Sheldon Ave., Houghton; ☎ (906) 482-2500.

Hancock Bike Shop, 115 Quincy, Hancock; ☎ (906) 482-5234.

Cross Country Sports, 507 Oak St., Calumet; ☎ (906) 337-4520

Travel Information

Keweenaw Peninsula Chamber of Commerce, ☎ (906) 482-5240.

Keweenaw Tourism Council, ☎ (906) 337-4579 or ☎ (800) 338-7982.

The Copper Country Tour includes Five Mile Point Road, which skirts the beautiful Lake Superior shoreline from Eagle River to Sand Hill Lighthouse at Five Mile Beach. The 23-mile ride is rated for intermediate and advanced riders due to the rugged hills of the Keweenaw Peninsula.

Copper Country Tour

County: Keweenaw
Starting Point: Amheek
Distance: 23 miles
Terrain: Hilly
Highlights: Five Mile Point Beach
Suggested Riders: Intermediate to advanced

Michigan's Copper Country is Keweenaw Peninsula, the site of the country's first mineral rush in the 1840s, and today the furthest you can drive from southern Michigan without leaving the state. A good 10-hour drive from Detroit, this unique region is often more familiar to residents of Wisconsin, Minnesota and Illinois than cyclists from Michigan. But it's well worth the effort of hauling those bikes this far north in order to enjoy one of the richest areas of the Midwest, in terms of both history and scenery. A lot like Wisconsin's Door County, only far less developed, the Keweenaw can be a beautiful ride, a place where around every bend are small towns, rocky beaches and breathtaking scenery.

This is the second of two Copper Country rides and makes for a 23-mile tour that begins in the small burg of Amheek, north of the college town of Houghton. The route was recommended by the staff of the Cross Country Sports in Calumet, one of the best bike shops in the peninsula. The route lets you enjoy the natural splendor of the region without as much work as the Brockway Mountain Tour.

Stage one (9.3 miles) Start this tour in the little town of Amheek and park at the Streetcar Station, a sandwich and ice cream shop. Head north on US-41, which can be busy although there are paved shoulders and locals report that drivers are used to cyclists throughout the summer and fall. You pass a craft shop and tourist office on the left just before reaching the town of Mohawk at *Mile 1.2*. US-41 makes a couple of curves through a residential section and past the White House Motel, then straightens out and crosses the Gratiot River at *Mile 4.5*.

Beware of the logging trucks rumbling by, something rarely seen in southern Michigan. Enjoy the nice long downhill ride at *Mile 6.8* before reaching the small town of Phoenix at *Mile 8*. You pass by the West Branch of the Eagle River on the way to the junction of M-26. At *Mile 9.3* turn left onto M-26, where there is a small store for those who are thirsty or suddenly in need of a boost of energy.

Stage two (6.3 miles) Continue north on M-26, which features paved shoulders on both sides. You pass through a wooded section and then enjoy a long downhill with views of the Eagle River to the east. Be careful on the downhill, which curves to the right at *Mile 11*. M-26 levels out briefly and then goes downhill again on its way towards Eagle River.

At *Mile 11.4* is the intersection of M-26 and Five Mile Point Road. This tour heads west along Five Mile Point Road but take time to ride into Eagle River. You cross a beautiful wooden bridge that arches across Eagle River to enter the town. Eagle River was founded in 1843 and is located on the mouth of its namesake river. In town are food stores, the old-

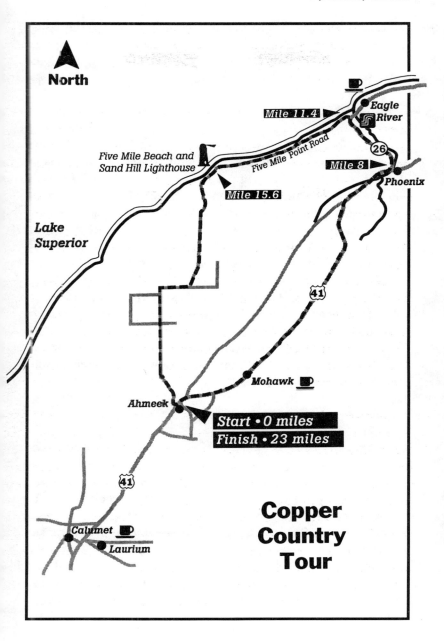

North

Mile 11.4

Eagle River

Five Mile Beach and
Sand Hill Lighthouse

Five Mile Point Road

Mile 8

Phoenix

Mile 15.6

Lake
Superior

41

Mohawk

Ahmeek

Start • 0 miles
Finish • 23 miles

41

Calumet
Laurium

Copper
Country
Tour

est courthouse in Michigan and Fitzgerald's, one of the finest restaurants north of Houghton that is dedicated to the freighter Edmund Fitzgerald. On the edge of town are the Eagle River Falls, definitely worth checking out.

Five Mile Point Road has no shoulders but is lightly traveled. There are great views of Lake Superior just before the road becomes hilly and enters a series of curves. Be prepared for the wind that can whip off of Lake Superior at times and make you reflect on the night the Edmund Fitzgerald sunk in 30-foot seas. There's a small roadside park at **Mile 13.7** before you enter a wooded stretch and pass the Lighthouse Inn on your right at **Mile 15.3**. Five Mile Point Agate Beach, a highlight of this tour, is just another third of a mile to the west. Time to park the bike and walk the steep path down to the sand and rocky beach that features a shipwreck site.

Stage three (7.6 miles) Continue riding up and down along Five Mile Point Road as it winds toward the south now. This includes a particularly long, steep uphill that crests at **Mile 17.7** and is followed by two sharp curves and some nice dips in the road. As you enter Amheek, turn left on Hubbell Street. You will pass a small park on your right at **Mile 23** before reaching the Streetcar Station on US-41 less than a quarter mile away.

Optional Rides: There are several options for additional mileage to this route. You can head south on US-41 and in less than 5 miles reach the historic mining town of Calumet. Once the richest city in Michigan, the entire downtown area of Calumet is now preserved as part of the Keweenaw National Historical Park and features stately churches, impressive mansions and its own opera house.

From Calumet you can follow a paved bike path 8 miles west along M-203 to McClain State Park. This 417-acre state park features a modern campground and almost 2 miles of Lake

Superior shoreline, where the sunsets are spectacular.

East of Eagle River is Sand Dune Drive, a road that rivals Brockway Mountain Drive for panoramic beauty. The 8-mile road connects Eagle River with delightful Eagle Harbor and along the way skirts high bluffs around Great Sand Bay. There is a gravel road that connects Eagle Harbor with US-41 to the south, but most cyclists either continue on to Copper Harbor via M-26 (see Brockway Mountain Tour) or simply backtrack on Sand Dune Drive to enjoy the stunning views and beaches a second time.

Bicycle Sales, Service

Dick's Favorite Sports, 1700 W. Memorial Dr., Houghton; ☎ (906) 482-0412.

Down Wind Sports, 520 Sheldon Ave., Houghton; ☎ (906) 482-2500.

Hancock Bike Shop, 115 Quincy, Hancock; ☎ (906) 482-5234.

Cross Country Sports, 507 Oak St., Calumet; ☎ (906) 337-4520.

Travel information

Keweenaw Peninsula Chamber of Commerce, ☎(906) 482-5240.

Keweenaw Tourism Council, ☎ (906) 337-4579, ☎ (800)·338-7982.

One of the most photographed spots in Michigan, Lake of the Clouds is the halfway point of a road route in Porcupine Mountains Wilderness State Park.

Lake of the Clouds Tour

County: Ontonagon
Starting Point: Union
Bay Campground
Distance: 19.7 miles
Terrain: Flat to rolling with a few
sharp uphills
Highlights: Lake of the Clouds, waterfalls
Suggested Riders: Intermediate

M-107 is a paved highway that begins near the Lake Superior shoreline but ends several hundred feet higher at one of the most photographed spots in the Midwest; the escarpment overlooking the Lake of the Clouds. From this popular observation point you can soak up the natural splendor of the rugged Porcupine Mountains in almost any direction. The center piece, however, is Lake of the Clouds, a 300-acre lake encased by steep ridges and peaks.

Black and white photos, even color ones, can't capture the beauty of Lake of the Clouds and its spectacular setting. You simply have to witness it yourself as thousands do every year with a trip to Porcupine Mountains Wilderness State Park. Best known as a hiker's paradise, this 60,000-acre park, the largest state park in Michigan, is the destination for a variety of activi-

277

ties including mountain biking, camping and downhill skiing in the winter. But don't forget the road bike. The paved roads on the perimeter of the park can be linked for a scenic route that combines cycling with ample opportunities to enjoy short hikes into the virgin pines the Porkies are famous for.

This can be a bike-and-hike tour providing visitors, especially families, an excellent introduction to the Porkies with stops at the Lake of the Clouds, the park's impressive Visitors Center and Union River Falls. Although you have to backtrack most of the route, the Porkies are worth it, especially Lake of the Clouds, one of Michigan's crowning jewels.

Fees: There is a vehicle entry fee at Porcupine Mountains Wilderness State Park. Cyclists who begin their ride within the park must obtain either a daily vehicle pass or an annual state park pass. To avoid this fee or to add mileage to the tour, begin in Silver City, located 2 miles west of the park entrance. Visitors entering the park on their bicycle do not pay an entry fee. There are additional fees if you want to camp at Union Bay. For a complete list of fees call the park headquarters at ☎ (906) 885-5275. To reserve a site in advance call ☎ (800) 44-PARKS.

Stage one (7.8 miles) The route begins off M-107 in the day-use area of the Union Bay Campground, the largest in the park with 99 modern sites. M-107 has gravel shoulders but also great views of Lake Superior and towering hemlocks. The entrance to the downhill ski area and chalet is quickly passed and then you begin climbing the first hill of the day, passing the trailhead to Government Peak Trail at *Mile 3.8* before crossing Cuyahoga Creek. Government Peak Trail extends south into the interior of the park but a walk of less than a quarter mile from M-107 puts you in the middle of a stand of 300-year-old pines.

At *Mile 4.5* you begin climbing a long, gradual hill that tops off at a picnic area overlooking Lake Superior, an excel-

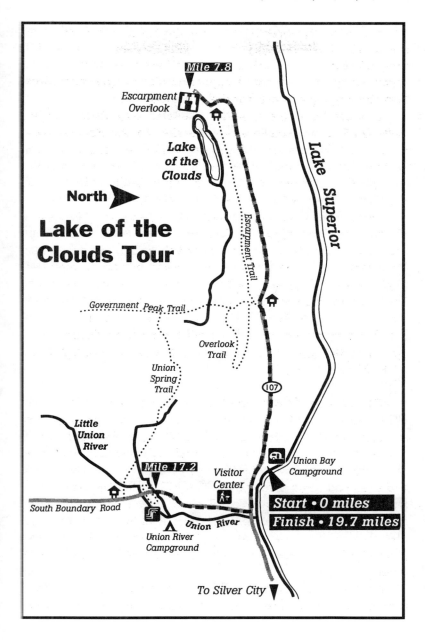

Mile 7.8

Escarpment
Overlook

Lake
of the
Clouds

North

**Lake of the
Clouds Tour**

Lake Superior

Escarpment Trail

Government Peak Trail

Overlook
Trail

Union
Spring
Trail

107

**Little
Union
River**

Mile 17.2

Visitor
Center

Union Bay
Campground

South Boundary Road

Union River

Union River
Campground

Start • 0 miles
Finish • 19.7 miles

To Silver City

lent place to catch your breath. The trailhead for the Lake Superior Trail is passed before the state highway ends at a contact station. Beyond it, the park road continues west, climbing a couple of steep hills before reaching the parking area of the Lake of the Clouds Overlook at **Mile 7.8**.

You made it! The day-use area features picnic tables, restrooms and a paved walkway to the Lake of the Clouds escarpment, where it's possible to sit on the edge of this steep bluff and revel in the awesome scenery. At the east side of the day-use area is the trailhead for the Escarpment Trail. By hiking a few hundred yards along this foot path you can easily escape the crowds of tourists that gather at the overlook to enjoy additional views of Lake of the Clouds.

Stage two (9.1 miles) Backtrack M-107 to the east, only this time enjoy a free downhill ride much of the way. At **Mile 15.5** you turn left (south) onto South Boundary Road, which is bumpy at first but quickly smooths out. Within a third of a mile, turn left (west) onto the entrance drive of the park's Visitors Center.

This impressive facility has exhibits on the history of the Porcupine Mountains as well as its black bears, fauna, waterfalls and wildlife. There's also a small theater where a multiprojector slide presentation is given on demand and a three-dimensional relief map that explains why your legs are so sore right now. Outside are bathrooms, drinking water and the Visitor Center Nature Trail, a one-mile loop with interpretive signs. Hours for the center during the summer are 10 a.m. to 6 p.m. daily.

From the Visitors Center turn right and head south on South Boundary Road. At **Mile 16.8** you reach the short access road to Union River Outpost, a scenic and secluded campground of only three sites. Just before the campground, is an iron bridge across Union River and from the middle of it you can see a small series of waterfalls upstream. Hike a ski trail along the river to get a closer view of the cascades.

Back on South Boundary Road you reach the turn-around point at *Mile 17.2*, the trailhead for the Union Mine Trail. The one-mile hike is an interpretive trail with 17 posts that correspond to a brochure available from a box at the trailhead. The walk features the ruins of the oldest copper mine operation in the park, dating back to 1845, and more waterfalls in the Union River.

From the trailhead, backtrack north on South Boundary Road and then west on M-107 to return to the Union Bay day-use area and complete this 19.7-mile ride.

Travel information

Porcupine Mountains Wilderness State Park, ☎ (906) 885-5275.

Porcupine Mountains Promotional Chamber; ☎ (906) 885-5885.

Ontonagon Tourism Council; ☎ (906) 884-4735.

Western U.P. Convention & Visitor's Bureau; ☎ (906) 932-4850, ☎ (800) 272-7000 (out-of-state only)

Author Mike McLelland   (Photo by Alison Engling)

The Authors

Mike McLelland

When the author bought his first mountain bike in 1991 and ventured into the Cannonsburg State Game Area northeast of Grand Rapids, Michigan he knew he found a pastime to last a lifetime. Not since the days of banana seats, coaster brakes and milk crate ramps had he experienced the pure exhilaration and face-splitting grins that mountain biking provided. Wonderfully, it combined serenity, adventure, exercise, nature, goals and rewards - a kind of microcosm of life.

As a reporter living in Grand Rapids, each weekend McLelland would plan a trip to a trail in a new locale - Muskegon, Manistee, Ludington, Cadillac, Grayling, Mio, Onaway, Kalamazoo, Pinckney. Researching this book gave him an opportunity to explore the Upper Peninsula in a way few people have - by its mountain bike trails - and allowed him to combine his love of writing with his favorite hobby.

Now an editor for a newspaper chain in Macomb County, McLelland doesn't have as much time to explore the ribbons of single track throughout the state like he used to. But on his computer he has an excellent panoramic picture of his trusty steed alongside the Bruno's Run trail near Munising to remind him of his adventures. Even on the busiest days with deadlines hovering over him, McLelland can look at that picture and be hundreds of miles away, swooping down some of the best trails in the Midwest.

Karen Gentry

A journalism graduate of Central Michigan University, Karen Gentry is based in Grand Rapids, Michigan and a frequent contributor of bicycling articles to various magazines and newpapers. She is also the author of *Cycling Michigan: The Best 25 Routes in West Michigan* and *Cycling Michigan: The Best 30 Routes in East Michigan*. This is her third book.